On the Intrinsic Value of Everything

On the Intrinsic Value of Everything

Scott A. Davison

continuum

Continuum International Publishing Group
80 Maiden Lane, New York, NY 10038
The Tower Building, 11 York Road, London SE1 7NX

www.continuumbooks.com

© Scott A. Davison, 2012

All rights reserved. No part of this book may be reproduced, stored in a retrieval system, or transmitted, in any form or by any means, electronic, mechanical, photocopying, recording, or otherwise, without the permission of the publishers.

ISBN: 978-1-4411-7792-6 (hardcover)
      978-1-4411-6282-3 (paperback)

Library of Congress Cataloging-in-Publication Data
A catalogue record of this title is available from the Library of Congress.

Typeset by Newgen Imaging Systems Pvt Ltd, Chennai, India

Contents

Preface	vii
Introduction	1
1 Preliminary Matters	9
2 The Possibilities	27
3 The Bearers	45
4 The Cutoff Question	61
5 Degrees	79
6 Ethics	99
7 Theism and Intrinsic Value	115
Bibliography	133
Index	145

Preface

Ideas belong to communities. I have been privileged to enjoy high quality philosophical conversation for many years in communities rich in ideas. It would be very misleading to suggest that I am solely responsible for the ideas presented in this book. I have learned many things from many people. Some played a part in developing these ideas through casual conversation, others provided helpful comments concerning papers or chapter drafts I had written or presented at conferences, and still others influenced me through their own writings. I am grateful to all of them, but especially to the following persons for reading earlier drafts of the material that appears here: Michael Bergmann, Thomas P. Flint, Michael Losonsky, Trentor Merricks, Gerald Twaddell, Wendell O'Brien, Wang Yafeng, Jack Weir, Wu Mowen, Yan Mengyao, Yang Xi, and two anonymous readers for Continuum Press. Special thanks are due to Ben Bradley, Phil Goggans, Gregory Mellema, Mark Murphy, Yujin Nagasawa, Xu Yingjin and Michael Zimmerman, who read a draft of the entire manuscript and provided me with very helpful comments that improved the final version in many respects. Thanks also to Amanda Hankinson for creating the final versions of the diagrams.

Work on this project was supported by a one semester sabbatical leave of absence and three summer research fellowships from Morehead State University, for which I am grateful

I owe a debt of gratitude to my parents and grandparents, who tried to teach me to value things properly. Finally, I am especially grateful to Rebecca Davison, who made it possible for me to work on this project during a special period of time that included the births of our three children. This book is dedicated to the four of them, Becky, Benjamin, Andrew, and Grace, who have taught me more about intrinsic value than they will ever realize.

Introduction

It is a beautiful day today. It is warm and sunny, the sky is blue, and the trees are healthy and green outside of my office window. Think about the universe and all of the things that it contains, given what you seem to know about them; what do you think about all of these things? Do you think that these things are good, or bad, or neutral? When I think about them, I find myself thinking that they are all good in some basic way. I don't mean that they have economic value (although some of them do), or that they have sentimental value (although some of them do), or that they are useful for achieving some purpose of mine (although some of them are); I mean that they are just good in themselves, period, independently of their relations to me or to people in general or to anything else at all.

In this book, I provide a philosophical exploration, explanation, and defense of this idea that everything that exists is good in some basic way. My Main Conclusion is that every concrete particular thing that exists is intrinsically valuable to some degree. This position is typically ignored in discussions of intrinsic value, perhaps because it is viewed as "radically implausible" or "heroic."[1] Defending it in a culture like ours, in which human interests almost completely dominate disputes about how to live in the world, must seem rather quixotic to some people. In fact, when presenting this material to audiences at conferences, I have felt like Socrates trying to persuade the younger Athenian jurors of his innocence after years of belief to the contrary.

I do my best in this book to defend the Main Conclusion using the tools of my trade, argument and analysis. But it does seem to me that this truth, if it is indeed a truth, is more properly felt or experienced

---

1 See Sober 1986, p. 243, and Norton 1992, p. 214, respectively.

in direct contact with the world than reached as the outcome of a series of abstract arguments. Perhaps works of fiction or poetry could be more effective in helping people to feel this truth, but I am not the right person to approach things in those ways.[2]

I do not try to demonstrate, in a noncircular way, that any specific thing is intrinsically valuable, since there is no way to do this. Instead, I develop arguments that appeal to widespread beliefs about the value of human beings, theoretical simplicity, and hypothetical thought experiments. But my case for the Main Conclusion does not rest on these arguments alone; I also try to exhibit the attractiveness of a certain picture, engaging in what Gary Gutting calls "persuasive elaboration."[3]

Gutting analyzes carefully some of the most influential developments in twentieth century analytic philosophy, including those due to Quine's rejection of the analytic/synthetic distinction, Kripke's elaboration of a causal/historical theory of naming and reference, various noteworthy epistemological developments in response to the Gettier problem, and so on. He argues that they owe their widespread influence not to specifically identifiable sound arguments, but instead to the persuasive elaboration of alternative pictures.[4] Gutting says that:

> The mere fact of developing a claim in some detail may serve to persuade us of its plausibility. Since more detail is likely to lead to problems, particularly when ideas are extended beyond their original domain, the more thoroughly and extensively a claim is developed without encountering problems, the more likely it is to be correct.[5]

In this book, I develop my Main Conclusion in detail without encountering significant problems, and this provides some evidence in its favor.

---

2 Wendell Berry certainly is—his essays, novels, and poems on behalf of respecting nature are far more compelling than anything I could ever write.
3 See Gutting 2009, pp. 77–8.
4 Gutting 2009, Chapter 4.
5 Gutting 2009, p. 77.

Here are the four claims that are central to this book, presented in the order of my (decreasing) confidence in them:

(1) Something is intrinsically valuable to some degree.
(2) Some concrete particular thing is intrinsically valuable to some degree.
(3) All concrete, particular things are intrinsically valuable to some degree. (This is my Main Conclusion.)
(4) Something in every exemplified ontological category is intrinsically valuable to some degree.

I defend all of these claims in the chapters that follow, but not equally. I defend (1) and (2) together, and without much argument, in Chapter 2. Without (1) or (2), the other claims could not be true. I admit freely that I cannot demonstrate them; I take the falsity of (1) to be the main alternative to the view developed in this book. I defend (3) in Chapters 2 through 5, and I defend (4) in Chapters 3 and 5.

Here is one way to think about my general approach to these questions. (This is intended to be an intuitive gesture designed to provide an overview of the big picture, not a detailed argument.) The cryptic ancient philosopher Heraclitus apparently said that "Corpses should be thrown away more than dung."[6] I think he's wrong about this. Of course, maybe he didn't really intend to endorse the literal meaning of these words; his ancient contemporaries called him "The Riddler," after all. Perhaps he really meant to say that the soul is more important than the body, or some such thing. In any case, where possible, it seems clear to me that corpses deserve to be treated with respect.

But corpses are not the only things that deserve this—living persons, animals, and plants also deserve to be treated with some measure of respect, along with paintings, buildings, places, symbols, natural formations and events. In all of these cases, there is some human-centered reason for treating the thing in question with respect. Typically this reason is related to some predictable,

---

6 See Heraclitus 1954, fragment 31.

well-known consequences for human beings. For example, one reason for treating corpses with respect is that the way we treat corpses is connected to the way we treat living human beings. But in addition to this human-centered reason for treating things with respect, there is another reason, a very different one. This is the intrinsic value of the thing in question. Roughly speaking, and just for now, let's say that something has intrinsic value if and only if it is good in itself, so that it ought to be valued for its own sake, independently of its relations to any other things.

There are different kinds of value, and people value things in different ways, sometimes appropriately and sometimes not. The lenses of my glasses are transparent and have a certain curvature that enables me to see clearly. This makes them highly instrumentally valuable to me, because I need to see clearly in order to do many things. But my glasses are not very sentimentally valuable to me, because I am not attached to them, and they are not very economically valuable, either.

By contrast, my father's glasses do not enable me to see clearly when I am wearing them; they are valuable to me in a different way. They are sentimentally valuable to me, because they belonged to my father, who is no longer alive. As it happens, they are not very economically valuable.

By contrast again, the glasses that once belonged to Michael Jackson are economically valuable, but not sentimentally valuable (to me, at any rate). They would be instrumentally valuable to me if I owned them, but not because they would help me to see; instead, they would be useful for me to own because of their economic value.

According to the picture that I develop and defend in this book, part of what it is to be a good person is to value the right things in the right ways and for the right reasons. I do not present here a complete account of what this involves, but focus instead on valuing things for their own sake, because of their intrinsic value. Part of what it means to be good at valuing things is to be able to distinguish the different kinds of value that things might possess, and to be appropriately responsive to the value that one encounters in one's life.

It is difficult to do this well in a culture that systematically ignores certain kinds of value. As St. Augustine says,

> Reason judges in one way, custom in another. Reason judges by the light of truth, so that by right judgment it subjects lesser things to greater. Custom is often swayed by agreeable habits, so that it esteems as greater what truth reveals as lower. . . . Children would rather see a man die (unless it is someone they love) than their pet bird, especially if the man frightens them and the bird is beautiful and can sing.[7]

To use St. Augustine's terminology, in our culture it has become for us an "agreeable habit" to regard everything in the world (except for other people, and sometimes even them) as things to be used, placed at our disposal. This involves very little conscious choice on our part, of course; immersion in this kind of culture would have this effect on nearly anyone. But the debate over my Main Conclusion is not a completely abstract one, divorced from ordinary life; instead, it is a loaded issue. If all things are intrinsically valuable, as I shall argue, then we need to do a better job tracking this value.

More specifically, I shall argue that the intrinsic values of things provide us with reasons for treating them with respect even if the human-centered reasons for doing this happen to fail on a particular occasion. For instance, suppose that I am the last person on earth, that I am about to die, and that there will be no negative consequences for anyone (human, divine, or otherwise) of destroying Leonardo da Vinci's famous painting *Mona Lisa* from sheer boredom. Still I should not do it. Before I became the last person on earth, I had two reasons for not destroying the *Mona Lisa*: (1) the human-centered fact that destroying the *Mona Lisa* would have negative consequences for other human beings, and (2) the intrinsic value of the painting. Now I have only one

---

7 Augustine 1993, p. 82.

reason for not destroying the *Mona Lisa*, but it's still a good one, in the absence of any stronger reason to the contrary.[8]

Of course, if there were something to be gained from destroying the *Mona Lisa*, then my reason for not destroying it might be overridden. For example, if destroying the *Mona Lisa* would save my life somehow, then clearly I should destroy it. It all depends; good reasons are typically capable of being overridden by other good reasons. Here we must distinguish *conclusive* reasons for doing things (which determine what one should do, all things considered) from *overridable* reasons for doing things (which specify an initial presumption in favor of doing something, a presumption that can be overridden by stronger reasons to the contrary). The intrinsic value of a thing is an overridable reason for treating it with respect, however exactly that should be done.

Assume for the moment that human beings are intrinsically valuable.[9] Are there any significant differences between human beings and other animals that should lead us to conclude that animals are not intrinsically valuable as well? Well, there are some interesting differences to consider, and of course it all depends on what kind of animal we have in mind. On closer investigation, though, it turns out that it is impossible to draw a sharp distinction between human beings and other animals that would justify the claim that only human beings are intrinsically valuable. This is because those qualities that seem relevant to intrinsic value come in degrees and are present in non-human animals as well (and those qualities that only human beings possess seem irrelevant to intrinsic value).[10] But if human beings and other animals are intrinsically valuable to some degree, then what about plants? What

---

8 I disagree with Brennan's Kantian view that "we owe no respect, no duties, to any of Leonardo's work, but we do have duties regarding it, duties which are owed to the many people for whom his work is of immense symbolic power" (Brennan 1984, p. 45); see Chapter 6 below for my discussion of intrinsic value and respect. (An anonymous reviewer has pointed out that this raises a number of other questions about those to whom duties are owed, questions that I shall not discuss here.) However, as I shall explain soon (Chapter 1, Section 2), my view implies that the *Mona Lisa* is no more intrinsically valuable than a perfect copy of it.
9 I shall defend this assumption in Chapter 2.
10 The extended argument for this conclusion can be found in Chapter 4.

about things on the border between the living and non-living, like viruses? What about machines?

I shall argue that the most reasonable answer to all of these questions is "yes, these things are intrinsically valuable to some degree." And this leads to the further claim that we have an overridable reason for treating everything with respect.

Many people will regard my Main Conclusion as obviously false. They will point out that a grain of sand, for example, just is; it is not good, let alone intrinsically good. And so they do not value it for its own sake to any degree. My view implies that such persons are morally defective in some sense, perhaps along the lines described by St. Augustine earlier. Just to be clear, I am certainly no saint when it comes to valuing things properly. I have my share of this defect, even though I believe that every concrete particular thing that exists has intrinsic value to some degree. If I could flip a switch that would align my choices, dispositions, and values with my moral beliefs, then I suppose I would do so, but this kind of consistency is not an easy thing for most of us to achieve. Instead, most of us seem to be stuck with a noticeable lack of fit between our moral beliefs and our characters.[11]

There is a related problem that makes things even more complicated: even if we are confident in our abstract moral beliefs, it turns out to be a complicated matter to translate them into practical, specific action in a reliable way. One of the lessons that can be drawn from the history of moral philosophy is that simple rules are never completely reliable (and completely reliable rules are never simple!). I make no claim to provide a complete moral theory (or even an environmental ethic) in this book; my project is ambitious enough as it is. More specifically, I do not claim that having all of the facts about the intrinsic values at stake in a situation is sufficient, all by itself, to determine what one ought to do.[12]

---

11 "Happy is he who does not condemn himself in what he approves": St. Paul, Romans 14:22, NASB. For more on this, see the discussion of hypocrisy in Chapter 6. Of course, sometimes correct moral practices lead to improvements in moral beliefs, so perhaps it is good that we cannot just flip the switch described above.

12 I say more about these things in Chapter 6.

In addition, there are many debates and questions concerning the nature of intrinsic value that I shall not discuss in this book at all. I shall not try to produce a successful noncircular analysis of the phrase *intrinsic value*, for example, or to disentangle every important concept related to this one. I shall not address the question of whether all values can be reduced to intrinsic values, or attempt to provide a complete list of the types of value in the world. I shall not venture deeply into those important meta-ethical debates concerning moral realism that have dominated value theory for the past few decades.[13] I shall avoid taking a stand on metaphysical questions wherever possible, including questions about what kinds of ontological categories are exemplified in the world (in addition to concrete particular things). These are all interesting and important questions, and some of them are clearly relevant to the final verdict concerning my Main Conclusion, but I simply cannot do justice to all of them here.

In the attempt to create a highly readable treatment of these issues, I have done my best to refrain from displaying technical apparatus for its own sake.[14] I have confined to footnotes those detailed discussions of the literature that are not essential to the main argument. (This means that if you are not interested in this literature, you may skip the footnotes entirely and still follow the argument without any difficulty.) When they disagree with my conclusions, my fellow philosophers should have little trouble deciding exactly where we part ways.

Reflecting on the question of the intrinsic value of everything has led me to better ways of thinking about the world and living in it. I hope that you will have similar experiences as a result of working through these issues, even if you end up disagreeing with my conclusions.

---

13 Although some areas of analytic philosophy have largely escaped from the long shadow cast by verificationism, value theory still seems to me to require a measure of liberation on this front; hopefully I can contribute to this process in a small way here.
14 This is something of an occupational hazard among analytic philosophers, and I confess to having done it myself on occasion.

1 Preliminary Matters

The concept of intrinsic value has a long and distinguished history, and like most philosophically interesting concepts, it has generated its share of controversy. I have little to add to the detailed debates about the proper elucidation of this concept. Instead, my focus is to argue that the concept has much wider application than most people have previously thought. But before I can argue for this conclusion, I should like to discuss briefly what would count as a successful account of the concept of intrinsic value, and then explain my own approach.

In *Rediscovering Colors*, Michael Watkins observes that a successful metaphysical account of colors must be semantically serious, ontologically serious, and epistemologically serious.[1] Similarly, we should require that a successful account of intrinsic value be all of these things, plus one more. By way of clarification, a semantically serious account of intrinsic value should respect the linguistic conventions governing the use of the phrase *intrinsic value*. An ontologically serious account should be compatible with what we seem to know about the world.[2] And an epistemologically serious account should explain how we might know (or at least justifiably believe) truths about intrinsic value. In addition, unlike a successful account of colors, a successful account of intrinsic value should be ethically serious in the minimal sense that its truth would have some clear bearing on how we should live our lives.

---

[1] See Watkins 2002, pp. 13ff. There may be other criteria for a successful account, of course, or at least other things we might like a successful account to do, but these criteria articulate minimally necessary conditions for a successful account.

[2] And not just on the basis of science: see Chapter 2 for more on this question.

I shall address the requirement of semantic seriousness first, in Sections 1 through 3 of this chapter, before touching on epistemological concerns briefly in Section 4. Then I shall defend the ontological seriousness of my account of intrinsic value in Chapters 2 through 5, arguing that it is more plausible than any alternative view. Of course, in the final analysis, judgments about ontological seriousness are difficult holistic judgments, so people are bound to disagree about them; such is the nature of philosophy. In Chapter 6, I shall defend the ethical seriousness of my Main Conclusion.

1. The Concept of Intrinsic Value

It is safe to say that there is a lot of disagreement concerning the nature of intrinsic value in the philosophical literature.[3] I shall not attempt to settle most of these disputes, let alone argue that my way of understanding the concept of intrinsic value is the best one. Instead, I shall introduce some helpful distinctions that others have drawn in order to explain my approach as clearly as possible. Providing an adequate survey and classification of the many ways in which philosophers have used the phrase *intrinsic value* would require writing another book, so I shall mention here only those distinctions that I find helpful in explaining my own approach.

Christine Korsgaard argues that there are two distinctions in goodness which are often conflated.[4] First there is the distinction between *intrinsic* and *extrinsic* goodness: something is intrinsically good if and only if it is good in itself, whereas something is extrinsically good if and only if it receives goodness from another source. By contrast, there is the distinction between things which are *sought for their own sakes* (ends or final goods) and things which are *sought for the sake of something else* (instrumental goods). She notes that people often define one half of one of these distinctions in terms of one half of the other distinction. For example, people

---

3 In fact, according to a number of authors, there is more than one distinct concept of intrinsic value: see Carter 1979, Feldman 1998, Kagan 1998, and Bradley 2006, for instance.
4 Korsgaard 1983, p. 170. There is much more to Korsgaard's important argument than I can respond to here, but see the discussion in Zimmerman 2001, p. 62.

often define the intrinsically good as that which is sought for its own sake. Korsgaard is right to point out that this is a conflation of the two distinctions, and it should be avoided. Since this book is about intrinsic value, I am interested in intrinsic goodness (as opposed to extrinsic goodness), not in whether things are actually sought for their own sakes (as opposed to actually sought as a means to further ends).

Another helpful distinction is drawn by Gary Watson. There is a difference between valuing something and desiring it, since a person can desire something without valuing it (or without valuing it to the same degree that it is desired). This happens in cases of impulsive desire, like the case of the fleeting desire of the humiliated loser in a sporting event to kill the gloating opponent, and in cases of estranged desire, like the case of the man who wishes for religious reasons that he had no sexual desire (but experiences it nonetheless).[5] Watson's distinction undercuts any straightforward attempt to define intrinsic value in terms of desire.

The distinctions introduced by Korsgaard and Watson imply that many of the standard descriptions of intrinsic value are inadequate.[6] For example, we cannot say that for something to be intrinsically valuable is for it to be desired for its own sake. We cannot even say that for something to be intrinsically valuable is for it to be valued for its own sake, and this for two reasons: first, not everything that is valued for its own sake need be intrinsically valuable. Second, not everything intrinsically valuable need be valued for its own sake. It is possible to have false negative experiences and false positive experiences of intrinsic value.

So something is intrinsically valuable if and only if it is good in itself, independent of its relations to other things. Clearly, I am not using the word *good* here in the sense of "useful for attaining some further end," since that would involve an appeal to instrumental value, not intrinsic value. I am not using the word *good* here in the sense of "good member of a kind," as in the sentence *This is a good*

---

5 Watson 1982, pp. 100–1.
6 For a few prominent examples, see William Frankena 1973, pp. 81, 86, and Zimmerman 2001, pp. 79–83.

axe, which attributes to some specific axe the distinctive virtues of being an axe (those that correspond to its conventional function, such as being sharp, well-balanced, and so forth).[7] So what *do* I mean by *good* when I say that something is "good in itself"?

Perhaps there can be no plausible, noncircular analysis of this sense of *good*.[8] Fortunately, it is not necessary to have such an analysis in order to understand what a word means.[9] Although I have no analysis to offer, I can exhibit an interesting logical connection between *intrinsically valuable*, as I use this phrase, and the valuing activities of fully informed, properly functioning valuers. Here it is: something is intrinsically valuable (or good in itself) if and only if it would be valued for its own sake by fully informed, properly functioning valuers.[10] So the claim that human beings are intrinsically valuable, for example, implies that human beings would be valued for their own sake by all fully informed, properly functioning valuers, whether they be human, divine, angelic, alien, or whatever.[11]

---

7 But see the discussion of the Thomistic approach to degrees of intrinsic value in Chapter 5. The origin of this approach lies in Aristotle: see *Nicomachean Ethics*, book I, chapter 7, 1097b, 24.

8 Perhaps I am using the word "good" in a basic, primitive, unanalyzable sense. For those who believe that Aristotle famously showed long ago that the word "good" cannot be used in this way, see the defense of Platonism in Adams 1999, pp. 38–40; for those who believe that Peter Geach and Judith Jarvis Thomson have recently shown the same thing, see the reply in Zimmerman 2001, chapter 2. G. E. Moore argued that there is just such a sense, of course, by means of his famous "Open Question Argument" (see Moore 1903, pp. 15–16); critical discussions of Moore can be found in Frankena 1973, chapter 6, Mackie 1986, chapter 2, Flanagan 1991, pp. 53ff, Scanlon 1998, pp. 96ff, Sayre-McCord 1988c, Zimmerman 2001, chapter 4, and Hurka 2005.

9 It is also fortunate, as Robert Adams notes, that we can be competent users of the word "good" without knowing the ultimate nature of goodness itself (Adams 1999, p. 16).

10 For similar claims, see O'Neill 1992, pp. 117–18, Anderson 1993, pp. 2–3, Zimmerman 2001, pp. 105ff and Rabinowicz and Rønnow-Rasmussen 2004. Of course, you and I are not fully informed, properly functioning valuers; in Chapters 2 and 5, I shall say something about this.

11 An anonymous reviewer has pointed out that there could be creatures who were not designed to understand or value certain kinds of things; if this were so, then one could be a properly functioning valuer without properly valuing everything that is intrinsically valuable. I shall ignore this complication in what follows, assuming that the standard for the intrinsic value of X is what valuers would value who are capable of understanding and valuing things like X.

The concept of a fully informed, properly functioning valuer clearly has a number of interesting implications. It includes both epistemic and normative components. On the epistemic front, a fully informed valuer would know all the relevant facts concerning a thing and possess a clear understanding of the different kinds of value (economic, instrumental, sentimental, intrinsic, etc.). On the normative front, a properly functioning valuer would have had proper training in the activity of valuing (if necessary[12]), a history of proper reflection on the objects of value, a properly disinterested stance that is focused on the object in question, and so forth.

Of course, if we were to take this claim about the relationship between intrinsic value and a fully informed, properly functioning valuer to be an *analysis* of the meaning of *good in itself* or *intrinsically valuable*, then it might involve some degree of circularity, since the normative aspect of *good* would reappear under the guise of "proper" function. (If we did not know what *good* meant to begin with, would we know what *properly functioning* meant?) As Rabinowicz and Rønnow-Rasmussen say, concerning a related suggestion, this kind of approach to analysis "will never leave the realm of value."[13]

But this is neither surprising nor damaging. Not only does the same problem arise for any plausible attempt to define other legitimate normative notions (such as the notions of duty, obligation, permission, right, etc.), but we encounter this kind of explanatory circle in other places too. For example, the physically possible is that which does not conflict with the laws of nature; the laws of nature tell us what is physically necessary; the physically necessary is that whose denial is not physically possible.[14] At some point, we must

---

12 In Chapter 7, I discuss the idea that the traditional theistic God would be a fully informed, properly functioning valuer, although God would not require any training in the activity of valuing things.

13 Rabinowicz and Rønnow-Rasmussen 2004, p. 421. For more complete discussions of the problems facing an analysis along the lines suggested, see D'Arms and Jacobson 2000 and the reply in Rabinowicz and Rønnow-Rasmussen 2004.

14 For a similar circle involving the notions of function and kind, see Murphy 2001, pp. 29ff. For a fascinating discussion of the lessons to be drawn from Quine's famously unsuccessful search for a noncircular definition of "analytic" in "Two Dogmas of Empiricism," see Gutting 2009, chapter 1.

take certain notions as basic; perhaps the primitive, undefinable sense of *good* is an acceptable starting point for this inquiry.

Different starting points have been suggested, of course. For example, G. E. Moore suggests defining the intrinsically good in terms of our duty to choose something,[15] C. D. Broad employs the notion of a fitting object of desire,[16] and both Roderick Chisholm and Michael J. Zimmerman appeal to what would be required in contemplation.[17] Other examples could be cited here, but the ones I have mentioned above are sufficient to make my point, which is that rather than eliminating the normative component, these approaches simply relocate it. There seems to be no plausible analysis of intrinsic value that can escape from the circle of normativity, but we should not find this troubling.

2. The Ground of Intrinsic Value

John O'Neill points out that when people say that something is intrinsically valuable, sometimes they mean simply that it has a kind of mind-independent value.[18] This raises a meta-ethical question about the source of intrinsic value, a question that is independent of the view that anything actually has any intrinsic value.[19] In response to this question, I reject "subjectivism" about value, the view that "the source of all value lies in valuers—in their attitudes, preferences and so on."[20] This is a very controversial topic; I don't have much to say about it here, but I will say just a few things.[21]

---

15 Moore 1912, p. 66.
16 Broad 1930, p. 283, cited in Lemos 1994, p. 8.
17 Chisholm 1986, pp. 52–3, Zimmerman 2001, pp. 107ff.
18 O'Neill 1992, p. 106. This is one of the three senses of "intrinsic value" that O'Neill distinguishes. (Thanks to Michael Losonsky for emphasizing to me the importance of O'Neill's arguments at an early stage of my project.) Unfortunately, O'Neill's two descriptions of objectivism are inadequate, since neither sense can accommodate cases in which someone's valuing something intrinsically is itself intrinsically valuable (Nozick 1981, p. 430); see O'Neill 1992, p. 112. My formulation avoids this difficulty.
19 O'Neill 1992, p. 109.
20 This is O'Neill's formulation: see O'Neill 1992, p. 106.
21 The little that I am about to say here is a clarification of my position, not a defense of it. I shall say more about this question in Chapter 2, in connection with the possibility that nothing in the world is intrinsically valuable at all.

Some of the value in the world comes from the valuing activities of valuers, but not all of it does. Phenomenologically, the experience of valuing something is an experience of responding to a feature of the world that is independent of one's valuing experience, not an experience of infusing something with value by taking up attitudes towards it. And sometimes this appearance is not misleading. As W. D. Ross says, with respect to actions in particular,

> It is surely a strange reversal of the natural order of thought to say that our admiring an action either is, or is what necessitates, its being good. We think of its goodness as what we admire in it, and as something it would have even if no one admired it, something that it has in itself.[22]

It is commonplace to assert that we do not encounter the world as it is in itself, but we do encounter the world in value experiences.[23] To what kinds of qualities of things do we respond when we have value experiences?

Following Thomas Scanlon's lead (but not in every respect), I endorse a version of the "buck passing" account according to which being intrinsically valuable is a matter of having intrinsically natural properties that would give any fully informed, properly functioning valuer good reasons to value something for its own sake.[24] Scanlon says that such features give *us* reasons to value things, but given my discussion above, I have recast his suggestion in terms of fully informed, properly functioning valuers.[25]

---

22 Ross 1930, p. 89 (quoted in Sayre-McCord 1988b, p. 20). For critical discussions of these issues, see Blackburn 1985a, Mackie 1986, Nagel 1986, and Sayre-McCord 1988b. The classic exposition of the view that Ross criticizes here can be found in Hume 1987, Book III, part I.
23 For a discussions of the concept of a "readymade" world, especially in light of arguments from Putnam and Kant, see Wolterstorff 2010.
24 See Scanlon 1998, pp. 96–8 and Nagel 1986, pp. 144ff. Unlike Scanlon, I restrict the properties in question to intrinsic ones, since I am talking about intrinsic value. For the distinction between a property's being intrinsic ("global") and an object's having a property intrinsically ("local"), see Humberstone 1996 or the brief summary in Weatherson 2007.
25 See the discussion of potential versus actual reasons in Dancy 2005, p. 43.

By contrast, according to one interpretation of Moore's highly influential account, when things have the right natural properties (that is, properties that can be specified without reference to any normative notions), they also have the additional property of being intrinsically valuable, which then gives us a reason to value them for their own sakes.[26]

Scanlon points out that the "buck passing" approach to goodness and value in general is supported by at least two considerations. First, whenever we consider particular cases, the reasons we have for reacting favorably to things are always based on its natural properties. For instance, the pleasantness of a resort leads us to recommend it, and the implications of a scientific discovery lead us to applaud it. Second, there seems to be no single property that could be the basis of all of our reasons for valuing the many and diverse things that we find to be good or valuable.[27]

It seems to me that Scanlon is right. The approach that I have outlined here implies that if there is any intrinsic value in the world, then it is objective and mind-independent, to answer O'Neill's meta-ethical question.[28] It also has the welcome implication that if any two things possess the same natural properties intrinsically, then they must be intrinsically valuable to the same degree. This means that the property of being intrinsically valuable is well-behaved and nonmagical, which is a necessary condition for being ontologically serious.[29] But what kinds of natural properties are relevant to the intrinsic value of a thing? Must they be intrinsic properties, as people have traditionally assumed?

---

26 Scanlon 1998, p. 97ff. This interpretation of intrinsic value is similar to the usual interpretation of colors and other so-called secondary qualities. See the discussion of this approach in O'Neill 1992, pp. 112–14, and the discussion of relational accounts of color in Watkins 2002, chapter 3.
27 These two advantages are discussed in Scanlon 1998, pp. 97–8.
28 At least in O'Neill's weak sense of objectivism: see O'Neill 1992, p. 112.
29 For interesting discussions of the supervenience of the moral on the natural, see Blackburn 1985, Mackie 1986, part 1, Boyd 1988, Forrest 1988, Lemos 1994, chapter 1, Feldman 1998, Scanlon 1998, chapter 4, and Zimmerman 2001, chapters 3 and 4.

Some authors have argued that we should depart from this tradition.[30] Shelly Kagan discusses cases in which we might think that the nonintrinsic properties of things, such as uniqueness, can make them intrinsically valuable. For example, he claims that the pen used by Abraham Lincoln to sign the Emancipation Proclamation might be intrinsically valuable by virtue of having played a special role in history.[31] I find these arguments strained at best, though. The instrumental value, the sentimental value, and the market value of Lincoln's pen are surely affected by its having played this special role in history, but not its intrinsic value.[32] So I shall follow the tradition here by insisting that the only properties relevant to intrinsic value are intrinsic properties. What is an intrinsic property, then?

It turns out to be surprisingly difficult to provide a successful analysis of this concept. Intuitively speaking, an intrinsic property of an object is one whose possession depends only on the object, not on anything distinct from it. One way to explain this idea involves the notion of a duplicate.[33] Imagine a device that could produce an atom-for-atom copy of any material object without

---

30 See Korsgaard 1983, Kagan 1998, Elliot 1992, Hurka 1998, Rabinowicz and Rønnow-Rasmussen 1999, and O'Neill 1992. These arguments may represent a concession to John Dewey's complaint that intrinsic value is an illusion because it abstracts away from all relations: see the discussion in Carter 1979, pp. 35–6, or Rolston's tiger on the moon (Rolston 1994, p. 174), or Tolhurst's description of a possible world that is "as empty as possible" (Tolhurst 1983), or the discussion of "lonely" objects and "contractions" (Weatherson 2007).

31 Kagan 1998, pp. 283–6. It is worth noting that by "intrinsically valuable", Kagan means "valued as an end, not as a means" (see Kagan 1998, pp. 230ff and the discussion in Rabinowicz and Rønnow-Rasmussen 1999).

32 Zimmerman (2001, pp. 37ff) and Bradley (2002, pp. 25–9) trace the apparent intrinsic value of these objects to states of affairs involving them instead. For more on this, see the discussion of the bearers of intrinsic value in Chapter 3, Section 2.

33 What follows is just an intuitive explanation, not an analysis; see the clear and helpful discussion of this in Weatherson 2007. For more on intrinsic properties and duplication, see Lewis 1983, Lewis 1986 (Section 1.5), Sider 1996, Vallentyne 1997, and Langton and Lewis 1998. The duplication approach does not apply to states of affairs, states of concrete objects, etc., but see the discussion of the Ambitious Speculative Conclusion in Chapters 3 and 5.

altering the original in any way. If my watch were duplicated by this machine, then there would be a new watch in the world, exactly like mine, and it would have all of the same intrinsic properties as the original.[34] The two watches would not have all of the same nonintrinsic properties, though, such as the property of having been owned by me for some years (only the original watch would have this property) or the property of being three feet away from my original watch (which only the duplicate watch could have).[35] So let us say that intrinsic properties are those properties that duplicates must share,[36] and let's say that the *intrinsic structure* of a thing is the set of properties that it possesses intrinsically.

3. Necessity, Change, and Existence

This description of intrinsic properties brings us to another aspect of the traditional approach to intrinsic value, namely, the idea that if something is intrinsically valuable in one situation, then it must also be intrinsically valuable in any other situation in which it might exist. More precisely, propositions of the form "X is intrinsically good" are often claimed to be necessarily true if true at all. This is sometimes called "universality" or "incorruptibility" or "essentiality."[37] Should we accept this thesis about intrinsic value?

Generally speaking, intrinsic properties need not be essential properties, so there is no reason to expect in advance that this thesis is true. In fact, there is a good argument for its falsity.

---

[34] This would be true at first, but over time, the watches would start to differ as the effects of differences in their distinctive environments began to accumulate. Here and throughout the book, I am talking about qualitative intrinsic properties, not identity properties or haecceities (see the discussion of this in Sider 1996, pp. 4–6).

[35] If it turns out that there can be two or more objects in the same place at the same time, then they will have the same degree of intrinsic value at that time (see the discussion of this in Lowe 2002, chapter 4, or Wasserman 2009).

[36] More precisely: property P is possessed intrinsically by X at time T if and only if it is (metaphysically) impossible for any other object Y to be a duplicate of X at T and to lack P at T.

[37] "Universality" is the preferred choice of Noah Lemos (see Lemos 1994, p. 11), "incorruptibility" belongs to Fred Feldman (see Feldman 1998, p. 346), and "essentiality" is the term used by Michael Zimmerman (see Zimmerman 2001, p. 63).

Philosophers have often assumed that intrinsic value is an all-or-nothing affair that does not admit of degrees, but this seems to be a mistake.[38] When reinterpreted in terms of degrees of intrinsic value, the thesis in question here amounts to the claim that "X is intrinsically good to degree D" is necessarily true if true at all. But this claim seems to be clearly false, since objects can change significantly in ways that affect their intrinsic value. The famous statue of Winged Victory, for example, is less intrinsically valuable now than it was long ago, when it still had a head. The dying insect outside of my window is less intrinsically valuable than it was yesterday when it was still fully alive. My eight year old son is more intrinsically valuable today than he was when he was just a fetus,[39] and so on. From this it follows that the specific degree of intrinsic value of a thing need not be an essential property of it.

Of course, by appealing to these cases, I have assumed that concrete particular objects can be bearers of intrinsic value. I shall defer my defense of that assumption to Chapter 3, where I shall begin to argue that the contemporary debate over the ontological status of the bearers of intrinsic value has failed to consider seriously the possibility that they can be found in every ontological category that is exemplified. I shall call this the Ambitious Speculative Conclusion,[40] to distinguish it from the Main Conclusion of the book (namely, the view that all *concrete particular things* are intrinsically valuable to some degree). For now, I shall simply assume that it is possible that some concrete particular object be intrinsically valuable, which is sufficient to ground my objection to the claim that the intrinsic value of something must be essential to it.[41]

---

38 See the discussion of this point in Chapter 2, and the discussion of degrees of intrinsic value in Chapter 5.
39 Or so it seems to me—not to say that fetuses have no intrinsic value at all; see Chapter 5.
40 As for my Main Conclusion is not ambitious and speculative enough!
41 Of course, my argument also assumes the commonsense view that concrete particular things can have different properties at different times, but I cannot explore here the philosophical controversy surrounding that assumption.

In order for something to be intrinsically valuable, it must exist.[42] So no purely fictional entities can be intrinsically valuable. And if the pile of rocks in my back yard[43] does not exist, then it cannot be intrinsically valuable, either, even if the individual rocks arranged in that way are intrinsically valuable when considered by themselves.

I have no general account of the nature of existence to offer here, or criteria that would help us to make decisions in difficult cases. Nor shall I discuss debates about exactly what exists or whether composition or existence might be vague. Instead, I shall assume the commonsense view that in addition to persons like you and me, there exist medium-sized physical objects like tables and chairs and plants and animals.[44] If this assumption turned out to be false in part, then some of the examples I discuss would be irrelevant, but the Main Conclusion of the book could still be true (for whatever particular things did exist).

This completes my discussion of the concept of intrinsic value. I have not addressed every interesting debate concerning the proper understanding of this concept, to be sure, but I have said enough to begin to develop the central arguments of the book. By way of summary, then: something is intrinsically valuable to a certain degree if and only if its intrinsic structure would lead fully informed, properly functioning valuers to value it for its own sake to that degree.

---

42 As Yujin Nagasawa has reminded me, this point emerged clearly from Kant and Russell's criticisms of St. Anselm's famous ontological argument for God's existence; see Anselm 1962, Kant 1933, and Russell 1905 and 1946.

43 Or my family or my nation or the water in the pool: see the interesting discussions of this in O'Neill 1992, pp. 115–17 and Merricks 2001.

44 I realize that this assumption is controversial in some circles, but I cannot discuss it in any detail here. For a lively discussion of these matters, see Merricks 2001. My arguments presuppose an ontology of objects and properties; for a gesture in the direction of an ontology of natural quantities instead, see the intriguing position sketched in Weatherson 2006.

4. Epistemological Seriousness[45]

Now that I have explored the contours of the concept of intrinsic value, I can say something informative about the epistemology of intrinsic value. Our epistemic access to the intrinsic value of particular things depends upon our epistemic access to their intrinsic structures, which typically involves the process of forming beliefs about those things based upon sense perception.[45] For example, imagine that in trying to catch a lizard in my house, by accident I pull off its tail. Suppose that a week later, I notice the same lizard again, and observe that it is growing a new tail. I have discovered something interesting about the lizard's intrinsic structure, namely, that it has the ability to regrow its tail. It may not be good for me that the lizard possesses this property (although it is clearly good for the lizard), but I might come to value the lizard, for its own sake, based on its possession of this property. The wonder that many people experience when they learn about the natural world seems to fit this pattern.

On the basis of this kind of experience, I might conclude that the lizard is intrinsically valuable to some degree. But how can I check the reliability of this kind of belief forming process?[47] Why should we think that having such experiences justifies anyone in believing anything about the intrinsic value of things?

One way to respond to this challenge would be to cite similar experiences which led to the formation of similar beliefs regarding similar objects, but of course this will not satisfy the skeptic about intrinsic value. The skeptic will point out that reference to similar

---

45 For another discussion of the epistemology of value along similar lines, see Adams 1999, chapter 15. My discussion is designed only to address the minimal requirements for epistemological seriousness, since the focus of this book is primarily ontological and ethical.

46 Providing an account of epistemic access to abstract objects is a burden that the believers in such entities must bear, so I shall not discuss it here.

47 I use the language of "reliability" (and the closely related language of "belief-forming process") as convenient shorthand for whatever epistemic values the skeptic cares about, but I do not intend to signal any allegiance to the reliabilist program in epistemology by doing so.

experiences simply pushes the question back a step: Why assume that those experiences were veridical, either? It seems impossible to argue for the reliability of any process that leads to beliefs about value without assuming, at some point, that we have access to some reliable process of this kind.

As one might expect, recent work in epistemology related to the notion of epistemic circularity has shown that this problem is not confined to processes that lead to beliefs about value. William Alston argues that a similar kind of circularity infects sense perception in general, as well as introspection, memory, and reasoning.[48] Some epistemologists have argued that we must accept epistemic circularity in some contexts or else face radical skeptical conclusions.[49] Here I shall assume the general reliability of sense perception, and argue that Alston's defense of the formation of religious beliefs on the basis of religious experience can be adapted to defend the formation of beliefs about intrinsic value on the basis of experiences like the one involving the lizard described above.

Alston argues that the practice of forming beliefs about the external world on the basis of sense perception and the practice of forming beliefs about God on the basis of religious experience are epistemically on a par.[50] One of his main arguments for this conclusion involves the notion of epistemic circularity mentioned above, namely, that there are no noncircular ways of establishing the objective reliability of either epistemic practice. When we try to check the validity of a particular perception of a physical object, for instance, we must appeal to other particular perceptions and general principles derived from them, thereby presupposing the general reliability of the practice that we are trying to check. In the same way, when religious people try to check the validity of a particular religious experience, they must appeal to other particular

---

48 Alston 1986.
49 See Alston 1986, Bergmann 2009, and the interesting critical discussion of these issues in Lammenranta 2011; see also the discussions of contextualism in Lewis 1996, Black 2006, Rysiew 2007, and DeRose 2009.
50 See Alston 1982, 1986 and 1991. Here I shall summarize briefly some of Alston's views without defending them; I cannot do his arguments full justice here. (They do not presuppose that God actually exists, incidentally.)

religious experiences and general principles derived from them, once again presupposing the general reliability of the practice that they are trying to check.

Of course, there are important differences between these two epistemic practices, as Alston and his critics have pointed out.[51] For example, forming beliefs about the external world on the basis of sense perception seems to be a universal practice, whereas forming beliefs about God on the basis of religious experience seems to be restricted to a limited number of persons. But as Alston points out, these differences are exactly what one would expect to see if the conclusions typically drawn from religious experience were correct.

It is instructive to compare the practice of forming religious beliefs in light of religious experience to the practice of forming beliefs about the intrinsic values of things on the basis of value experiences. There is no noncircular way to show that any particular experience of intrinsic value is correct; instead, we must appeal to other value experiences and general principles derived from them. Perhaps this is the kernel of truth in John Stuart Mill's much maligned "proof" of the Greatest Happiness Principle, which involves the claim that pleasure is good because it is desired.[52] It is also worth pointing out that the practice of forming beliefs about intrinsic value on the basis of value experiences is subject to a number of theoretical constraints and possible defeaters, just like the practice of forming religious beliefs on the basis of religious experience.[53]

Robert Nozick identifies a number of theoretical constraints. He argues that whatever makes things intrinsically valuable, it must impose an ordering condition on things, valuing it must be itself valuable, disvaluing it must itself be disvaluable, and so on.[54] These constraints, together with our considered judgments about particular cases and general principles reached through reflective equilibrium, provide possible defeaters for apparent

---

51 Perhaps the most penetrating of Alston's critics is Paul Draper (1992).
52 Mill 1969, p. 61.
53 As Alston notes: see Alston 1982.
54 Nozick 1981, chapter 5, Section 1.

experiences of intrinsic value. This is important because not every value experience is veridical, just as not every religious experience is veridical.[55]

I have said that if human beings are intrinsically valuable, then a fully informed, properly functioning valuer would value me on the basis of my intrinsic structure. A fully informed, properly functioning person would regard my annihilation as a significant loss. But there is no way to verify that this is so without appealing to other particular judgments concerning intrinsic value. We have no independently verifiable, general criteria that could be used to correlate sets of properties possessed intrinsically with degrees of intrinsic value. So we must appeal instead to our shared intuitions about what is worthy of being valued for its own sake, which are themselves shaped by a number of factors.

To a great extent, our value experiences are constrained by the ways we have been taught to regard various kinds of things and experiences.[56] People from some non-Western cultures have an advantage here, I believe, because they are taught to value more things for their own sakes from an early age, which permits them to have a wide range of value experiences that are not available to the typical Western person. For example, consider the following description from Robert E. Carter:

> Whereas we in the West try to get clear about our concepts, struggle for abstract generalizations where the atmosphere is purest, and analyze in great detail, the Japanese sit and concentrate on a raindrop, or on nothing at all, finding in it

---

[55] Erazim Kohák describes the experience of seeing clearly that existence *per se* is positively good in an encounter with the moon on a cold winter night (Kohák 1984, pp. 60–2). Without dismissing this out of hand, I confess that it seems puzzling to me how one might reach this kind of conclusion on the basis of this kind of experience.

[56] See Adams 1999, pp. 359ff for a discussion of Alston and the social nature of what Adams calls "evaluative doxastic practices." My overall project is similar in some respects to Adams's, although his is much more broad, ambitious, Platonic, and theological than mine (not to mention more nuanced in execution). For critical discussions of Adams, see Chapter 4, Section 3, and Chapter 7, Section 1.

the synthesis of all things, and forgetting about the rest of the world while rejecting analysis as an unacceptable and distorting act in the presence of such beauty and meaning.[57]

Even though Carter's description almost certainly does not fit the typical Japanese person, he is pointing to a real cultural difference that makes a difference. A person who believes that mundane things like raindrops can be sources of value experiences probably has a head start in the direction of appreciating properly the intrinsic value of everything.[58] By contrast, those of us who have been taught since childhood that nearly everything we encounter in everyday life is value neutral may have a more difficult time here.

5. Conclusion

I shall not attempt to demonstrate, in a noncircular way, that any particular thing is intrinsically valuable. I will develop several arguments that appeal to widespread beliefs concerning the intrinsic value of human beings, and I will argue that my conclusion is more plausible on theoretical grounds than the alternative possibilities. Of course, I will also engage in the persuasive elaboration of my picture, hoping that you will agree with me that it can be extended in detail without encountering serious problems. In order to do these things in the rest of the book, though, I need to attend to a number of other preliminary matters.

First, I will need to identify the logical possibilities for intrinsic value and to defend the claim that it comes in degrees; this I shall do in Chapter 2. Then I shall discuss the contemporary debate concerning the bearers of intrinsic value in Chapter 3, arguing that both concrete particular things and abstract objects can be intrinsically valuable. Chapter 4 will be devoted to a critical

---

[57] Carter 1979, p. 47; compare this to the catalogue of mostly Western "Voices of Natural Piety" in Walhout 1978. See also the fascinating comparison in Motokawa 1989.
[58] Yujin Nagasawa has pointed out to me that some non-Western traditions also embrace pantheism or panpsychism, each of which probably entails my Main Conclusion (although the converse does not hold).

discussion of attempts to answer the Cutoff Question by drawing a plausible, nonarbitrary distinction between that which is intrinsically valuable and that which is not. In Chapter 5, I shall provide an account of degrees of intrinsic value, applying it both to concrete particulars and to abstract objects. Chapter 6 will be devoted to the ethical seriousness of the Main Conclusion. Finally, in Chapter 7, I shall ask how the existence of God might make a difference to any of these conclusions.

2 The Possibilities

In Chapter 1, I explained how I shall understand the concept of intrinsic value in this book. In this chapter, I explore the logical possibilities for intrinsic value in the world and present some reasons for thinking that just one of them obtains.

1. Dimensions of Possibility: A Number of Questions

What are the logical possibilities for intrinsic value in the world? It is important to distinguish the different dimensions of possibility that must be considered. First, there is the question of how much of the world (if any) is intrinsically valuable; let's call this the Distribution Question. (The Main Conclusion of this book answers the Distribution Question in the following way: "Everything, to some degree.") Second, there is the question of whether intrinsic value is an all-or-nothing affair or a matter of degree; let's call this the Degree Question. Third, there is the question about what kinds of things, ontologically speaking, might be the bearers of intrinsic value; let's call this the Question of the Bearers of Intrinsic Value.

I postpone the Question of the Bearers of Intrinsic Value to Chapter 3, where it can receive the careful discussion that it deserves. I address the Degree Question in this chapter, but before I do that, I need to explain briefly some additional complications that arise in connection with the Distribution Question.

One question that is closely related to the Distribution Question, but not identical to it, could be called the Cutoff Question, which is: if some kinds of things are intrinsically valuable and others are not, then where is the cutoff point between them? Closely related to the Cutoff Question, but not identical to it, is the Explanation Question, which is: what explains why a given intrinsically valuable thing is intrinsically valuable?

I argue in Section 5 of this chapter that in one sense, the Explanation Question can be answered, and that in another sense, it need not be. As for the Cutoff Question, I argue in Chapter 4 that providing a nonarbitrary answer to it seems to be impossible, and that this fact, together with the account of degrees of intrinsic value developed in Chapter 5, constitutes an argument for the conclusion that everything that exists is intrinsically valuable to some degree. But before I develop these arguments, I wish to address the Degree Question.

2. The Degree Question

By way of reminder, here is the Degree Question: can intrinsic value come in degrees, or must it be an all-or-nothing affair? Many people seem to assume without explicit argument that intrinsic value must be an all-or-nothing afffair.[1] I find this assumption puzzling; nothing said about the nature of intrinsic value in Chapter 1, for instance, implies (or even suggests) that it must be an all-or-nothing affair. It is difficult to address the reasons behind this assumption if they are not given explicit formulation. In this section I consider one argument for this assumption and then offer my best conjectures about what other people might be thinking when they assume that intrinsic value must be an all-or-nothing affair. In each case, I explain why these ways of thinking are not plausible.

Tom Regan claims that if X and Y are both inherently valuable, then they must be inherently valuable to the same degree.[2] He argues for this view in the following way:

> What could be the basis of our having more inherent value than animals? Will it be their lack of reason, or autonomy, or intellect? Only if we are willing to make the same judgment in the case of humans who are similarly deficient. But it is not true that such humans—the retarded child, for example, or

---

[1] See Anderson 1997, p. 97, and the interesting discussion of degrees of intrinsic value in Bradley 2006.

[2] Although Regan's notion of inherent value is broader than my notion of intrinsic value, it includes something like my notion as a subcomponent, so I will ignore the differences in what follows; nothing of substance turns on this difference here, as far as I can tell.

the mentally deranged—have less inherent value than you or I. Neither, then, can we rationally sustain the view that animals like them in being the experiencing subjects of a life have less inherent value. *All* who have inherent value have it *equally*, whether they be human animals or not.[3]

I am sympathetic to the strategy of Regan's argument here. We must not draw arbitrary lines. But there seem to be clear cases of differences in intrinsic value among experiencing subjects of a life, even if we cannot locate immediately the basis of those differences. A human being is more intrinsically valuable than a slug. But must we also "bite the bullet" here and say that the less than fully functioning human being is less intrinsically valuable, all other things being equal, than the fully functioning human being?[4]

I think that the answer here is probably "yes." But it is important to qualify this claim immediately. It does not follow that preferential treatment is appropriate for humans of higher intrinsic value. This is because in general, facts about intrinsic value do not settle questions about what we ought to do, all things considered. Considerations involving instrumental value might be part of an explanation of the importance of treating all human beings with equal moral consideration.[5] It does not follow that all fully functioning human beings are equally intrinsically valuable, or that our society's typical way of classifying the functioning of human beings "tracks" actual degrees of intrinsic value. Finally, we should not assume that human beings are at the top of the scale of intrinsic value; as I shall argue later, it might turn out that dolphins or aliens or some other kinds of things[6] are more intrinsically valuable than a fully functioning human beings.

---

3 Regan 1985, pp. 13–26; emphasis his.
4 See the excellent discussion of the general question of egalitarianism and the attempt to locate a nonarbitrary criterion for moral standing in Knapp 2007 (thanks to Ben Bradley for bringing this article to my attention). Adams tries to argue for egalitarianism and to answer the Cutoff Question all at once: see the discussion of Adams in Chapter 4, Section 3, and Chapter 7, Section 1.
5 For more on the question of the ethical implications of facts about intrinsic value, see Chapter 6.
6 Or God: see Chapter 7.

Returning to Regan's argument, once we recognize the possibility of degrees of intrinsic value in the first place, it should not be surprising that not all human beings are intrinsically valuable to the same degree. If intrinsic value varies by degrees depending on the properties that things possess intrinsically, then it seems more likely that no two human beings are ever intrinsically valuable to exactly the same degree. Hence Regan's argument for the conclusion that intrinsic value must be all-or-nothing is not persuasive.

Here is another possibility: perhaps those who assume that intrinsic value cannot come in degrees are implicitly reasoning in the following way:

Premise (P1). There is some satisfactory answer to the Cutoff Question, so that we can confidently distinguish those kinds of things that are intrinsically valuable from those that are not.

Premise (P2). Those kinds of things that are intrinsically valuable do not differ from one another with respect to any properties that (a) vary by degrees and (b) are clearly relevant to intrinsic value.

Conclusion (C). Therefore, if any two things are intrinsically valuable, then they are intrinsically valuable to the same degree.

As I indicated earlier, P1 is not plausible: we should not be so optimistic about answering the Cutoff Question (see Chapter 4). As I shall explain later, P2 is false, since human beings and other animals do differ from one another with respect to properties that vary by degrees and are clearly relevant to intrinsic value. So although this argument might be valid, it is unsound.

Here is a different way to argue for the conclusion that intrinsic value must be an all-or-nothing affair:

P1. There is no satisfactory answer to the Cutoff Question, so we cannot confidently distinguish those kinds of things that are intrinsically valuable from those that are not.

C. Therefore, if one thing is intrinsically valuable to a certain degree (such as a human being), then everything else must be intrinsically valuable to that same degree (such as bacteria or viruses).

Someone who reasons in this way might conclude further that since it is absurd that bacteria and viruses are intrinsically valuable at all, it follows that nothing is intrinsically valuable (by *reductio ad absurdum*).[7]

Although I have some sympathy for the view that nothing is intrinsically valuable at all (see Section 3), this way of trying to settle the Degree Question is obviously flawed. Even if P1 were true, it would not follow that all intrinsically valuable things were intrinsically valuable to the same degree. For it could be the case that even though we had no satisfactory answer to the Cutoff Question, we could still distinguish clearly different degrees of intrinsic value among intrinsically valuable things; we might think that a human being is clearly more intrinsically valuable than a snail. So this argument is clearly unsatisfactory.

Finally, it is possible that some of the people who assume that intrinsic value must be all-or-nothing are making additional assumptions about the nature of intrinsic value or using the phrase *intrinsic value* in a way that is importantly different from mine.[8] I can only recommend that they compare their approach to my approach in order to see which one seems more plausible.

Since I am aware of no further arguments for the conclusion that intrinsic value must be an all-or-nothing affair, I conclude that there are no good positive reasons for embracing this conclusion. But now consider the following claim:

Claim X: If both human beings and snails were intrinsically valuable, then human beings would be more intrinsically valuable than snails.

This claim has the form of a subjunctive conditional statement. For those who believe that it is impossible for anything to be

---

7 In this way, the Degree Question would be answered as well: everything would have the same degree of intrinsic value as everything else (namely, zero).
8 See Bradley 2006.

intrinsically valuable, it takes the form of a counterfactual conditional with an impossible antecedent.[9] But that doesn't prevent us from making a meaningful comparison between it and the following claim:

> Claim Y: If both human beings and snails were intrinsically valuable, then snails would be just as intrinsically valuable as human beings.

When I consider X and Y, I find that X is more plausible than Y, and this is so even on the assumption that it is impossible for anything to be intrinsically valuable at all. This strikes me as positive evidence, although rather weak and speculative evidence, for the conclusion that it is logically possible for intrinsic value to vary by degrees.

I conclude that there are no good reasons to think that intrinsic value must be an all-or-nothing affair, and perhaps some positive reason to think otherwise. I shall offer an account of degrees of intrinsic value in Chapter 5, after I have explored the Question of the Bearers of Intrinsic Value (in Chapter 3) and the Cutoff Question (in Chapter 4). For now, it is enough to conclude that it is possible for intrinsic value to vary by degrees. In what remains of this chapter, I shall discuss the Distribution Question and the Explanation Question, keeping in mind the possibility that intrinsic value varies by degrees.

3. Maybe Nothing is Intrinsically Valuable

What are the possibilities for the distribution of intrinsic value? First, it is possible that nothing in the world is intrinsically valuable to any degree. Let's call this "The Possibility of Complete Intrinsic Value Neutrality," which is depicted in Figure 1:[10]

---

9 Sometimes this kind of claim is called a "counterpossible"; see Zagzebski 1990 and Vander Laan 2004 for interesting discussions of the idea that such claims are not all trivially true, contrary to the received understanding of the semantics for counterfactuals involving similarity relations among possible worlds (based on the work of Lewis 1973 and Stalnaker 1968).

10 The heavy black line indicates the level of intrinsic value. The Figures discussed in this book are oversimplified for the sake of illustration, depicting only the possible degrees of intrinsic value of possible particular things relative

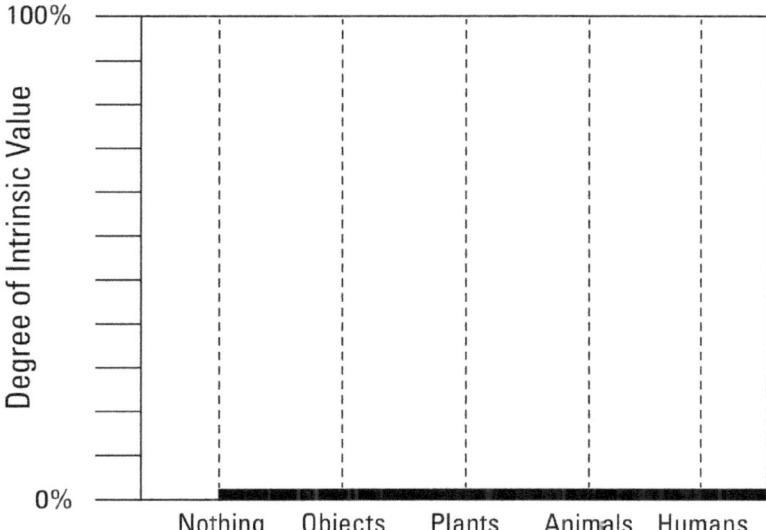
Figure 1 The Possibility of Complete Intrinsic Value Neutrality

Although I think that the possibility of Complete Intrinsic Value Neutrality does not actually obtain, it must be admitted that some considerations certainly point in this direction. It is a simple view, and simple views always have some theoretical appeal. In addition, not only would this view avoid ontological commitment to the existence of intrinsic value, but it would also provide a simple, principled answer to the Cutoff Question and the Explanation Question. These are important virtues to consider, virtues that some readers will probably find decisive.

Emrys Westacott argues for Complete Intrinsic Value Neutrality along some of these lines. He also claims that unless we have criteria that enable us to decide what is intrinsically valuable and what is not, we will be involved in the "unnecessary and unjustified

---

to one another, to emphasize my Main Conclusion. (See also Chapters 3 and 5 for more on the bearers of intrinsic value and a defense of the Ambitious Speculative Conclusion, according to which some bearer of intrinsic value can be found in every exemplified ontological category.)

positing of qualities and characteristics."[11] Comparing the concept of intrinsic value to the absurd notion of intrinsic (economic) price, he says that there is "no consideration which leads us to believe that the application of the concept of intrinsic value is any more reasonable or legitimate than the application of the concept of intrinsic price."[12]

I cannot answer Westacott's argument here by providing criteria that would enable us to distinguish the intrinsically valuable from the intrinsically neutral, since I believe that everything that exists is intrinsically valuable to some degree. He claims that "in the absence of criteria for deciding which things fall under it, the concept itself is empty, and its application blind."[13] In general, though, it seems doubtful that we need criteria in order to decide whether or not something falls under a given concept. We may be aware of paradigm cases, for instance, without having criteria.

For example, I have three young children: Benjamin, Andrew, and Grace. Although I have many other attitudes and desires connected with my children, most of which do not involve the concept of intrinsic value, I regard each one of them as being intrinsically valuable, and I can't imagine thinking otherwise.[14] As Peter Loptson says, while defending the claim that death is objectively bad,

> A human being is a magnificent piece of equipment. We can certainly be self-infatuated, *over* philanthropical (in an etymological sense), and speciesist. Yet it seems reasonable, and accurate to say: a fully functioning operational adult human being is a fine, fine bit of machinery, a splendid conjunction

---

11 Westacott 1994, p. 182.
12 Westacott, 1994, p. 183.
13 Westacott, 1994, p. 184.
14 It might be the case that for all persons P, P cannot help but act as if P is intrinsically valuable; this suggests a kind of pragmatic, Cartesian bootstrapping argument for the intrinsic value of (some) human beings (which I shall not pursue here). If readers find my example in this paragraph contentious, then they should feel free to substitute their own favorite case of knowing that something is F without having criteria for F-ness in order to answer Westacott's argument.

of cognitive and affective systems, working with amazingly elegant intricate harmony.[15]

A human being a fine bit of machinery because of its intrinsic structure. This structure grounds complex dispositions that set it apart from nearly everything else in the world, and would provide a fully informed, properly functioning valuer with reasons for valuing a human being for his or her own sake.

To illustrate this vividly, and to argue for it in a different way, consider what I shall call the Annihilation Test. Imagine that someone invented a machine that could annihilate something completely. Like talking about duplication (see Chapter 1, Section 2), talking about annihilation might strike some readers as extremely far-fetched, if not positively science-fictional. But recent experiments involving the isolation of antimatter suggest that an annihilation machine might actually become technically feasible some day.[16]

Imagine that there is an annihilation machine that works in the following way: something is placed inside the machine, the door is closed, a button is pushed, and the thing inside is completely annihilated, so that no part of it exists at all. A fully informed, properly functioning valuer would surely regard the machine's annihilation of one of my children as the loss of something valuable for its own sake. And since other children are like mine in the relevant respects, in order to be consistent I must also regard them as being intrinsically valuable, too. This doesn't mean that I will love the other children in the same way that I love my own children, of course, but it does mean that I will recognize them as falling under the same concept, the concept of the intrinsically valuable, even if I have no criteria for its application.

---

15 Loptson 1998, p. 140, italics his. Loptson also argues that the uniqueness of each person contributes to his or her intrinsic value (pp. 141ff), but given the view of intrinsic properties adopted in Chapter 1, this will be false, since a duplicate of X would not have the property of being uniquely like X. For more on this, see the interesting discussions in Weatherson 2007 and Sider 2003.

16 More importantly, this thought experiment is helpful for isolating the relevant issues, more helpful (it seems to me) than some well-known "isolation" approaches: see Carter 1979, pp. 35–6, Korsgaard 1983, pp. 175–7, and Tolhurst 1983.

Someone might wonder whether this thought experiment actually shows that my children are intrinsically valuable themselves, as opposed to facts about them (or states of affairs involving them or concrete states of theirs).[17] Imagine that we ask our fully informed, properly functioning valuer to distinguish all of these different kinds of things from one another. (Since the valuer is fully informed, this should not be a problem.) Then we can ask about them one at a time.

First, would the valuer regard the cessation of facts about my annihilated child as a loss of something valuable for its own sake? I think so, but not for the same reasons (and not to the same extent) that others might. Would the valuer regard the nonobtaining of various states of affairs involving my annihilated child as a loss of something valuable for its own sake? Again, I think so, but not for the same reasons (or to the same extent) that others might. Would the valuer regard the nonexistence of various concrete states of my annihilated child as a loss of something valuable for its own sake? Once again, I think so, but not for the same reasons (or to the same extent) that others might.

Finally, setting aside these other kinds of entities, we can focus exclusively on my annihilated child himself or herself: would our fully informed, properly functioning valuer regard the annihilation of this child as a loss of something valuable for its own sake? The fact that we answered "yes" to the three questions preceding this one seems to make no difference to me; it still seems that the answer here is "yes."[18]

Returning to the thread of the main argument: Westacott's demand for criteria that would enable us to distinguish the intrinsically valuable from the intrinsically neutral seems to be overly restrictive, since we are capable of making many judgments of this sort without appealing to criteria. He continues by insisting that at some point, "these objectivist concepts of

---

17 Ben Bradley raised this helpful point in correspondence.
18 See the discussions of the bearers of intrinsic value in Chapters 3 and 5, where I argue for the Ambitious Speculative Conclusion that bearers of intrinsic value can be found in all of these ontological categories.

intrinsic value, superiority, and obligation need to be converted into a currency we can actually use."[19] By "currency we can actually use," I suspect that he means something like "criteria whose application we can verify in some objective, independent, naturalistic, nonnormative way." But this is asking too much. How many other normative notions would pass this test?[20] What would happen to other perfectly respectable notions, like the notions of metaphysical possibility and necessity? Westacott's arguments for Complete Intrinsic Value Neutrality, like most arguments in this vein, would prove far too much if they were successful.

I have not considered here every argument that might be offered for the possibility of Complete Intrinsic Value Neutrality.[21] It would take too much time and space to do that, and in the end, I don't think that it would prove to be very helpful. Of course, I have no conclusive argument to demonstrate that the possibility of Complete Intrinsic Value Neutrality does not obtain. Such is the nature of philosophical inquiry, and I see no point in pretending otherwise. In the end, the possibility of Complete Intrinsic Value Neutrality seems to be the main competitor to the view that I defend in this book. I shall develop arguments that are intended to tilt the scales against it, but whether or not those arguments are successful must be left to each reader to judge. This completes my brief discussion of the possibility of Complete Intrinsic Value Neutrality.

4. Other Possibilities

A second possibility lies at the other end of the spectrum of possibilities, namely, the possibility that everything that exists is intrinsically valuable to the highest degree. Let's call this "The Possibility

---

19 Westacott, p. 184.
20 As Nagel says, "The claim that certain reasons exist is a normative claim, not a claim about the best causal explanation of anything" (Nagel 1986, p. 144). Westacott's complaint is reminiscent of positivism, and echoes the Western preference for things that can be measured or quantified; see the provocative Flowers 1998 and Adams 1999, p. 118.
21 Not surprisingly, they have never struck me as especially compelling. For a helpful introduction to this matter, see Nagel 1986, chapter 3.

of Complete Intrinsic Value Saturation"(see Figure 2). Like the possibility of Complete Intrinsic Value Neutrality, the possibility of Complete Intrinsic Value Saturation has certain theoretical virtues. It is simple, in its own way, and it provides a nonarbitrary answer to the Cutoff Question.

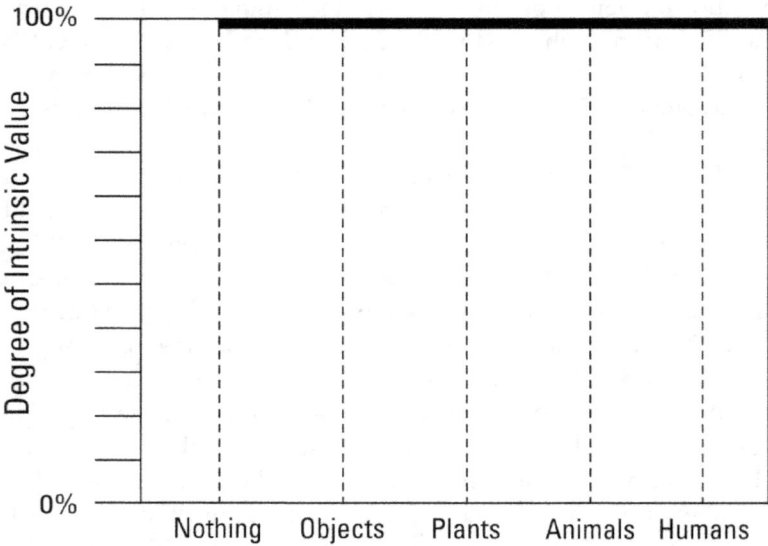

Figure 2 The Possibility of Complete Intrinsic Value Saturation

However, the possibility of Complete Intrinsic Value Saturation is highly implausible once we accept the fact that intrinsic value might come in degrees. Given the relative plausibility of claim X over claim Y noted above, one might wonder if a more plausible position could be found in between the possibility of Complete Intrinsic Value Neutrality and Complete Intrinsic Value Saturation.

As noted at the beginning of this chapter, there are two dimensions to consider here, and they might vary independently of one another: degree of intrinsic value, on the one hand, and distribution of intrinsic value, on the other. One way to locate a possibility in between the two extreme possibilities just discussed would be to modify the possibility of Complete Intrinsic Value Saturation by diminishing the *degree* of intrinsic value that it attributes to everything that exists, leaving unchanged its distribution of intrinsic value. Let's call this combination "The Possibility of Ubiquitous Intrinsic Value Varying by Degrees" (see Figure 3)

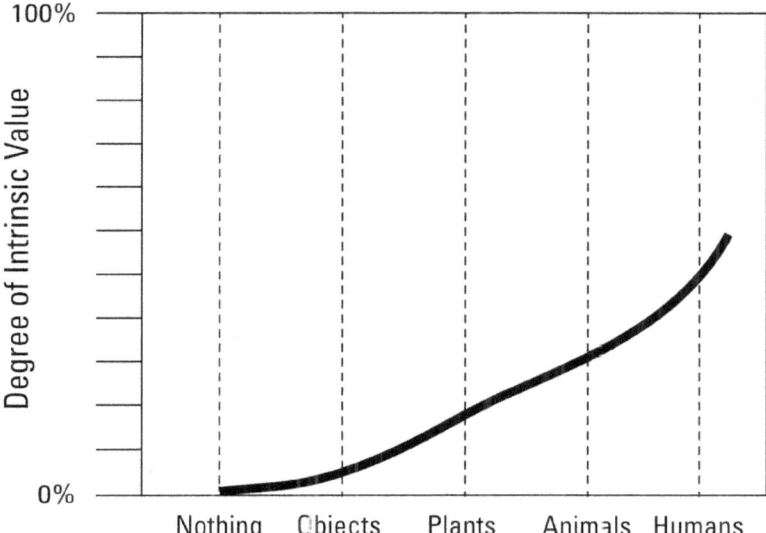

Figure 3 The Possibility of Ubiquitous Intrinsic Value Varying by Degrees

A second way to find a different middle position would be to diminish not the degree but the *distribution* of intrinsic value, to claim that some existing things are not intrinsically valuable at all; let's call this "The Possibility of Restricted Intrinsic Value of the Highest Degree" (Figure 4, following page).

Finally, a third way to find a middle position would be to do both of these things, resulting in "The Possibility of Restricted Intrinsic Value Varying By Degrees" (Figure 5, following page).

Is there any way to narrow down the range of plausible positions from among these three? Once we admit the possibility of degrees of intrinsic value, it seems more reasonable to suppose that not everything is intrinsically valuable to the same degree. The human being seems to be more intrinsically valuable than the slug, for instance.

40 On the Intrinsic Value of Everything

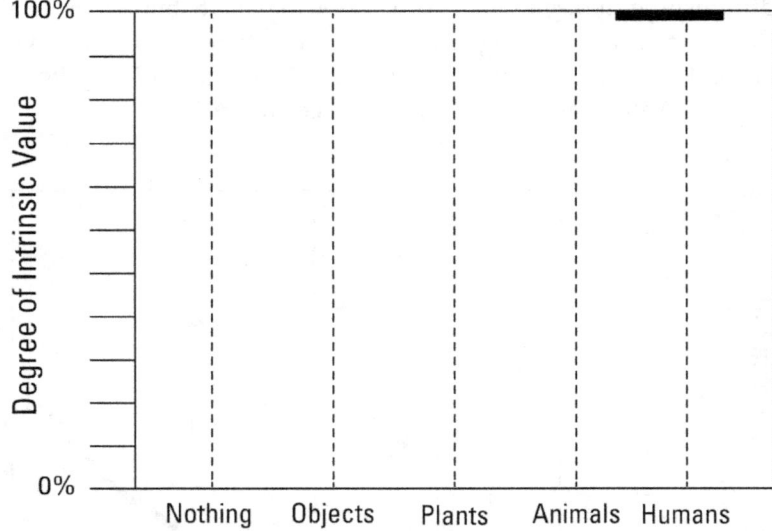
Figure 4 The Possibility of Restricted Intrinsic Value of the Highest Degree

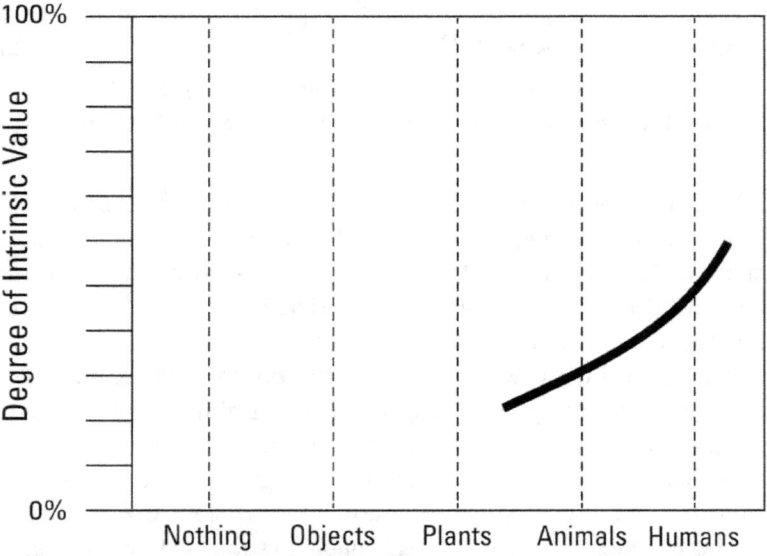
Figure 5 The Possibility of Restricted Intrinsic Value Varying By Degrees

So of these three new options, the first (the possibility of Ubiquitous Intrinsic Value Varying By Degrees, Figure 3) and third (the possibility of Restricted Intrinsic Value Varying By Degrees, Figure 5) seem to be the most reasonable ones. Of course, restricting the distribution of intrinsic value will raise the Cutoff Question in a very pressing way (see the abrupt ending of the line in Figure 5). This suggests that the possibility of Ubiquitous Intrinsic Value Varying By Degrees (Figure 3), which also happens to be my Main Conclusion, is the most plausible possibility of all. This completes my exploration of the logical possibilities under the heading of the Distribution Question.

5. The Explanation Question

Before turning to the question of the Bearers of Intrinsic Value (Chapter 3), together with a discussion of the Cutoff Question and its bearing on the possibilities just enumerated (Chapter 4), it will be helpful to investigate the Explanation Question. By way of reminder, the Explanation Question is this: what explains why intrinsically valuable things are intrinsically valuable?

Some authors suggest that if we cannot answer this question clearly, then our approach to the nature of intrinsic value must be mistaken.[22] In order to understand the Explanation Question, it is important to see what form a satisfactory answer might take. Suppose that we want to know why some particular thing X is intrinsically valuable. We might offer the following explanation:

(P1) Anything that possesses property P intrinsically is intrinsically valuable.

(P2) X possesses properties P intrinsically.

(C) Therefore, X is intrinsically valuable.[23]

---

22 See Bernstein 2001, especially pp. 337ff; Bernstein seems to assume that all value is value for something or someone else. By contrast, Elliot Sober offers an ethical argument for the necessity of answering the Explanation Question (Sober 1986, p. 242); see the discussion of this in Chapter 6, Section 1.

23 For the sake of simplicity, here I ignore various complications such as degrees of intrinsic value and the possession of multiple properties, each of which might vary by degrees.

If we knew that (P1) and (P2) were true, then perhaps this would enable us to understand the truth of (C). So perhaps this would count as a successful explanation of the intrinsic value of the particular thing, X. But this would leave unresolved another question, a question that would seem to be just as pressing as the original question about X: why is (P1) true? In other words, why is the presence of these properties correlated with intrinsic value in this way? And are these properties the only ones that are correlated in this way with intrinsic value?

In Chapter 1, I defended a Scanlon-style "buck passing" approach to intrinsic value, according to which a thing's being intrinsically valuable is just a matter of its possessing intrinsically various properties that would lead a fully informed, properly functioning valuer to value it for its own sake to some degree.[24] One of the reasons Scanlon offers in defense of this approach to value in general is that there seems to be no single property that could be the basis of all of our reasons for valuing the many and diverse things that we find to be good:

> [T]he fact that a resort is pleasant is a reason to visit it or to recommend it to a friend, and the fact that a discovery casts light on the causes of cancer is a reason to applaud it and to support further research of that kind.[25]

However, I shall argue in Chapter 5 that everything that exists has an intrinsic structure of some kind, and that this structure is the basis of degrees of intrinsic value; if I am right about this, then presumably we can answer the Explanation Question uniformly for all intrinsically valuable things in one fell swoop after all.[26]

There is a sense, though, in which even this kind of answer would not completely address every dimension of the Explanation

---

24 See Chapter 1, Section 9, and Scanlon's description in Scanlon 1998, pp. 96–8.
25 Scanlon 1998, p. 97.
26 Robert Nozick suggests instead that degrees of organic unity serve as the basis of all cases of intrinsic value, but he does not hold that all concrete particular things are intrinsically valuable; see Nozick 1981, chapter 15.

Question. Some people might claim that any reasonable explanation would involve the reduction of intrinsic value to natural, nonnormative properties and relations. Perhaps they would hold this view because of a meta-ethical position that they embrace, or because they think that all respectable explanations terminate by appealing to well-known and well-behaved properties (perhaps physical properties generally, or perhaps the sorts of properties revealed by the natural sciences), not by appealing to value properties.

I have very little sympathy for this kind of demand.[27] Let's set aside the "buck passing" account of intrinsic value for the moment and consider instead the Moorean alternative of an irreducible, nonnatural property of intrinsic value.[28] Why should we think, in advance of an inquiry into the nature of intrinsic value, that such value properties should turn out not to be fundamental features of the world? I know of no plausible arguments for this conclusion, even though many people seem to take it for granted. A number of other respectable features of our world are in the same position as intrinsic value here. At a certain point in our explanations, we reach that which cannot be explained any further, and I see no reason to insist that facts about intrinsic value are not things of this sort. As Thomas Nagel observes,

> If values are objective, they must be so in their own right and not through reducibility to some other kind of objective fact. They have to be objective *values*, not objective anything else.[29]

I conclude that in one sense, the Explanation Question can be answered, and that in another sense, it need not be. I am now in a position to discuss in detail the question of the Bearers of Intrinsic Value and the Cutoff Question in Chapters 3 and 4, respectively.

---

27 See Sayre-McCord 1988a, the helpful discussion of Moore's nonnaturalism in Hurka 2005, and footnote 20.
28 See the discussion of this in Chapter 1, Section 2.
29 Nagel 1986, p. 139, emphasis his. See also Murphy 2001, pp. 91ff., and Adams 1999, pp. 25ff.

3 The Bearers

Ontologically speaking, what kinds of things might be intrinsically valuable? Philosophers have argued for a number of different answers.[1] It is interesting to note that the current debate typically proceeds on the assumption that all intrinsically valuable things must belong to a single ontological category.[2]

Ben Bradley argues that unless fine-grained entities (like states of affairs) are bearers of intrinsic value, we will be unable to distinguish the fact that someone named Jeffrey is pleased (which we might regard as intrinsically valuable) from the fact that this same Jeffrey is pleased at his victim's unjust suffering (which we might regard as intrinsically bad). Bradley claims that "We certainly could not make such claims by attributing value to Jeffrey himself,"[3] and seems to take this as a reason for thinking that states of affairs are bearers of intrinsic value. But he seems to be assuming here without argument that attributing intrinsic value to persons would rule out attributing it to states of affairs as well. Is this a fair assumption?

In this chapter and in Chapter 5, I argue that this assumption is mistaken because some bearer of intrinsic value can be found in every ontological category that is exemplified. I call this the Ambitious Speculative Conclusion, to distinguish it from the Main

---

[1] For example, Roderick Chisholm, Noah Lemos, Ben Bradley and others prefer facts or states of affairs, Michael Zimmerman and Törbjorn Täannsjö prefer states of concrete objects, and Elizabeth Anderson and Robert Adams prefer concrete particulars.

[2] A few authors claim that certain theoretical virtues favor taking such an approach (e.g. Rabinowicz and Rønnow-Rasmussen 1999, pp. 44–5 and Zimmerman 2001, pp. 39ff.), but this is very rare—almost every author who discusses this question simply assumes that it is correct.

[3] Bradley 2002, p. 27.

Conclusion of the book as a whole (namely, that every concrete particular thing is intrinsically valuable to some degree). If the Ambitious Speculative Conclusion is correct, then many arguments in the current debate over the bearers of intrinsic value are beside the point.

In order to defend my Main Conclusion, I need not defend the Ambitious Speculative Conclusion, since the Main Conclusion is only about concrete particular things, not about any other ontological categories. This means that even if I am wrong about the Ambitious Speculative Conclusion, I still might be right about the Main Conclusion. But since the Ambitious Speculative Conclusion, if correct, represents a significant advance in the debate over the bearers of intrinsic value, it seems worth the trouble to defend it here.

I defend this conclusion in two stages. In this chapter, I respond to the most important negative arguments in the literature purporting to show that certain categories of things could not include bearers of intrinsic value. Here I ignore almost completely those positive arguments purporting to show that some category of thing could include bearers of intrinsic value, since those conclusions are all compatible with mine. In chapter 5, after I have provided an account of degrees of intrinsic value, I provide some additional, positive reasons for thinking that intrinsic value can be found in every exemplified ontological category.

1. Exclusionary Arguments Against Abstract Objects

Noah Lemos argues for the conclusion that abstract properties could not be bearers of intrinsic value. Instead, he holds that obtaining states of affairs (which he calls "facts") are the only bearers of intrinsic value.[4]

Following the example of Roderick Chisholm and others,[5] Lemos views states of affairs as necessarily existing, abstract

---

[4] His arguments can be found in Lemos 1994; unless otherwise specified, page references in what follows refer to this work of his. Lemos's terminology here echoes Ross's (see Zimmerman 2010).

[5] See Chisholm 1986 and Plantinga 1974, for instance. Zimmerman points out that Ross held a view similar to Lemos's, according to which only obtaining states of affairs ("facts") are intrinsically valuable (Zimmerman 2010).

entities, only some of which obtain. For example, the state of affairs of some human person's having walked on the moon obtains, but the state of affairs every human person's having walked on the moon does not. What explains this difference between obtaining and nonobtaining states of affairs? The existence and nature of concrete particular things explains why some states of affairs obtain and others do not (and not vice versa).[6] Lemos defines a fact as a state of affairs that obtains, and he argues that facts alone are the bearers of intrinsic value.

In criticizing the view that properties might be the bearers of intrinsic value, Lemos says the following:

> A world containing nothing that exemplifies properties such as wisdom, beauty, or pleasure, or that has no concrete particulars at all, would be a world without anything intrinsically good, even if it contained the abstract, unexemplified properties of wisdom, beauty, or pleasure.[7]

This claim seems false to me. Wouldn't each Platonic Form, even if it existed in an otherwise empty world, have a degree of intrinsic value all by itself?[8] What about a world containing only numbers, propositions, and sets? Such a world would seem to me to be better than a world containing absolutely nothing.[9] Even if I am wrong about these judgments, though, one thing seems quite clear: the outcome of Lemos's thought experiment here is not obvious at all. So this attempt to exclude properties as possible bearers of intrinsic value fails.

Furthermore, Lemos's criticism appears to count against his own favored view, the view that facts are the bearers of intrinsic

---

6 See Lemos 1994, p. 21, and the comparison between truth for propositions and obtaining for states of affairs in Plantinga 1974, pp. 47–8.
7 Lemos 1994, p. 23.
8 Plato certainly seems to have though so: see the discussion of this point below and in Chapter 5.
9 See Chapter 4, Section 3 for the development of an argument regarding concrete particular things that I shall call the "Anything is Better than Nothing" argument.

value. Since facts are (by definition) obtaining states of affairs, and states of affairs are abstract entities, there could be worlds containing no concrete particulars at all that nonetheless contained the same states of affairs as our world does. In our world, some of these states of affairs count as facts (because they obtain), and some of these facts are intrinsically valuable, according to Lemos; but in a world with no concrete particulars, these same states of affairs would exist and yet would have no intrinsic value, if Lemos's argument were sound.

Lemos considers such an argument, and replies that we must attend more carefully to the distinction between states of affairs and facts, where facts are states of affairs that obtain.[10] But facts differ from nonobtaining states of affairs only in virtue of the existence of the concrete, particular things to which they bear some relation (namely, the relation being exemplified by), so Lemos's reply here is puzzling. The concrete particular things in virtue of which states of affairs obtain seem to be doing all of the work, since they distinguish those states of affairs that are from those that are not.

An example will make this point more clear. Assume for the sake of argument that pleasure is intrinsically valuable, and imagine that some actual person Rose experiences pleasure from smelling a rose at a particular time t. Lemos might say that the state of affairs of Rose's experiencing pleasure from smelling a rose at time t is a fact (because it obtains), and that this fact is intrinsically valuable. But what distinguishes this obtaining state of affairs (or fact, as Lemos would say) from the very same state of affairs in a different possible world, a world in which Rose does not even exist? In this other world, the state of affairs in question exists, but it does not obtain; hence it is not a fact in that world. Why should we think that this state of affairs (or fact) is intrinsically valuable in our world, when it differs from the same state of affairs in another possible world only because it is exemplified by certain concrete particular things in this world? The value that Lemos attaches to

---

10 Lemos 1994, p. 25.

the obtaining state of affairs seems to come from the value of the concrete particular things, not vice versa.[11]

Incidentally, still other problems attach to Lemos's proposal that obtaining states of affairs are the only bearers of intrinsic value. States of affairs can be more or less general, and more than one state of affairs will obtain in virtue of a single arrangement of concrete particular things. The high specificity of some states of affairs is often cited as a virtue of the claim that states of affairs are the bearers of intrinsic value,[12] but there is no reason to insist that there cannot be general states of affairs as well. In terms of the example mentioned above, many states of affairs obtain in virtue of Rose's experiencing pleasure as a result of smelling a rose at a time t, including the following ones: Rose's smelling a rose at t, someone's smelling a rose, someone's smelling something, someone's experiencing something, and so forth. But some of these states of affairs could also obtain in virtue of what we people would typically regard as bad arrangements of concrete particular things. For example, the state of affairs of someone's experiencing something could obtain in virtue of one person's harming another unjustly; so should we count this obtaining state of affairs (or fact) as intrinsically good or bad?

If someone's experiencing something obtains in this world in virtue of Rose's smelling a rose (and nothing else), then by Lemos's lights it seems to be intrinsically valuable, but if this same state of affairs obtains in another world in virtue of someone's being harmed unjustly, then by Lemos's lights it seems to be intrinsically bad. Now it seems even clearer that concrete particular things are doing the work in determining intrinsic value. The conclusion to draw from all of this might be that if states of affairs have any intrinsic value at all, then it is the sort of intrinsic value appropriate

---

11 Zimmerman (2001, pp. 46ff. draws a similar conclusion regarding Chisholm's view, and also provides a more detailed (and perhaps more charitable) discussion of Lemos's reply (pp. 49–51). For more on this question, see the discussion of the intrinsic value of states of affairs in Chapter 5, Section 4.
12 See Bradley 2002, pp. 27ff, for example.

to abstract objects, and they all possess it to the same degree in all possible worlds in which they exist.[13]

At least one other person would join Lemos in rejecting my defense of abstract objects here. This is Elizabeth Anderson:

> Our basic evaluative attitudes—love, respect, consideration, affection, honor, and so forth—are nonpropositional. They are attitudes we take up immediately toward persons, animals, and things, not toward facts. Because to be intrinsically valuable is to be the immediate object of such a rational attitude, states of affairs are not intrinsically valuable if they are not immediate objects of such attitudes. Evaluative attitudes take up states of affairs as their mediated objects through the desires, hopes, wishes, and other propositional attitudes that express them.[14]

Anderson's distinction between the immediate and mediated object of our evaluative attitudes confirms my criticism of Lemos's view above. However, unlike Anderson, I do not hold that something is intrinsically valuable only if it is the immediate object of a rational, basic evaluative attitude. Restricting intrinsic value in this way is arbitrary and overly restrictive, so her conclusion to the effect that states of affairs cannot be intrinsically valuable strikes me as unwarranted.[15]

As for the question of the object of our basic evaluative attitudes, it is worth pointing out that some people have advocated taking such attitudes toward abstract objects. In Plato's Symposium, for

---

13 Or so I shall argue in Chapter 5.
14 Anderson 1993, p. 20. A similar argument is suggested in Adams 1999, p. 17, although it involves an appeas to a lack of unity in states of affairs that I will reject below (see Chapter 5, Section 4).
15 Robert Card argues that Anderson's argument here does not actually preclude intrinsically valuing all states of affairs connected with the objects of one's basic evaluative attitudes (see Card 2004, especially p. 262), and Nicholas Sturgeon argues that there is a way to reinterpret what Anderson says about our attitudes towards these objects in terms of our attitudes toward states of affairs involving them (see Sturgeon 1996, section III); thanks to Ben Bradley for bringing these papers to my attention.

instance, Diotima of Mantinea is depicted as recommending that the young Socrates advance from the love of particular persons through a series of steps (often called "the Ascent") to the love of the Form of Beauty itself.[6] Philosophers since Aristotle have routinely criticized Plato for postulating the existence of the Forms unnecessarily. But as far as I know, none has suggested that it would be a mistake to love the Form of Beauty if it existed.

Similar considerations apply to Michael Zimmerman's criticism of Panayot Butchvarov's view that properties are the bearers of intrinsic value. According to Zimmerman, "It is not properties such as happiness that are good but, again, their being instantiated that is good."[17] We need not choose between these two alternatives; instead, we should attribute some degree of intrinsic value to the property (if it exists) and some degree to the instantiations of the property (if they exist).

I conclude that there is no good reason to believe that abstract objects cannot be bearers of intrinsic value (if they exist). Although such things are not the typical objects of our rational, basic evaluative attitudes, as Anderson correctly notes, this does not suggest that they cannot possess intrinsic value on their own.[18]

2. Exclusionary Arguments Against Concrete Particulars

Lemos offers two arguments against the possibility that concrete particular things might be bearers of intrinsic value. His first argument begins with the plausible assumption that if any concrete particular things have intrinsic value, then human persons do. Then he argues as follows:

> I am skeptical that persons are bearers of intrinsic value. Imagine a world in which nothing is beautiful or wise or morally good, a world that contains no pleasure or pain, but

---

16 See *Symposium* 210e–212a; see also the middle books of Plato's *Republic* and the discussion in Vlastos 1973. Robert Adams argues that it is appropriate to love universals such as truthfulness (Adams 1999, pp. 158–60).
17 The views in question are found in Butchvarov 1989; Zimmerman's criticisms are found in Zimmerman 2001, p. 48.
18 For more on the intrinsic value of abstract objects, see Chapter 5.

contains persons in a deep, dreamless sleep, their bodies tended by machines, a world in which the only living things are these sleepers. . . . When we consider the question of intrinsic value, such a world seems to be without any intrinsic value; it does not seem to be a world that anyone should desire or favor in and for itself. The mere fact that there are persons in that world contributes no intrinsic goodness to it.[19]

Let's call the world in which these persons exist "The Sleeping World." What should we say about Lemos's argument here?

First, we are considering here the possibility that persons are bearers of intrinsic value, not worlds, but Lemos's conclusion seems to concern the intrinsic value of the Sleeping World as a whole. Even if we were to agree with Lemos that the Sleeping World as a whole is not intrinsically valuable (a conclusion we should resist, I think, if there exists such a thing as the Sleeping World), still this would not commit us to the conclusion that the persons who exist in the Sleeping World are not intrinsically valuable.[20]

What should we say about the persons who exist in the Sleeping World? To develop Lemos's story further, imagine that one of these sleeping persons is killed as a result of a malfunctioning maintenance machine. Would this involve the loss of something intrinsically valuable, even if nobody in the Sleeping World ever knew about it? I think so; this case seems parallel to the Annihilation Test described in Chapter 2. A fully informed, properly functioning valuer would surely regard the death of one of the people in the Sleeping World as a significant loss.[21]

Lemos's second argument for the conclusion that concrete particular things could not be bearers of intrinsic value concerns the

---

19 Lemos 1994, p. 28.
20 As Lemos points, out, we should not assume that the value of a whole is determined completely by the values of its parts (see Lemos, chapter 3); in addition, we cannot infer anything about the values of the parts using only information about the value of the whole.
21 An anonymous reviewer pointed out that our feeling of repugnance at imagining humans stuck in a deep unconscious state in Lemos's Sleeping World is best explained in terms of our belief that they are intrinsically valuable, and hence should not be treated this way.

objects of our basic evaluative attitudes. Contrary to Anderson, Lemos argues that the objects of such attitudes are states of affairs or facts or events:

> In ordinary contexts, when someone says, *I want a yacht*, what he wants, the object of his want, is not simply a yacht, but more precisely his owning or having a yacht.[22]

Things seem to be the same with respect to the attitudes of love and hate, Lemos suggests, quoting with approval Everett Hall's suggestion that *John loves Mary* is really elliptical in that "What John loves is Mary's having a pair of blue eyes, a dimple in her right cheek, a way of turning suddenly pensive in the midst of a playful mood, . . . etc."[23]

Lemos's argument here is not convincing. The patterns that emerge from our basic evaluative attitudes are not sufficient by themselves to determine facts about intrinsic value, including facts about its bearers. The example about the yacht might be a case in which a person wants to stand in a certain relation to a concrete particular thing, but not all basic evaluative attitudes are like this, as Anderson has argued persuasively. More importantly, just because a person wants to stand in a certain relation to a concrete particular thing, it does not follow that the person has no basic evaluative attitudes toward the thing in question; in fact, the latter may explain and justify the former.[24]

Furthermore, Hall's suggestion about the nature of love is also misleading in this context.[25] To use the memorable phrase coined by Robert Kraut, love is historical and "de re."[26] A distinction that is helpful here comes from John Brentlinger, who defends

---

22 Lemos 1994, p. 29.
23 Lemos 1994, p. 31.
24 See the discussion of Anderson in Card 2004, where it is suggested that both a concrete particular person and some states of affairs involving that person could be bearers of intrinsic value.
25 It is worth noting also that the relationship between loving something and finding it intrinsically valuable is not completely clear, despite the tendency to discuss them together (as in, for instance, Zimmerman 2001, pp. 41–5).
26 See Kraut 1986 and Anderson 1993, p. 20.

the Platonic conception of erotic love against the charge that it is impersonal. His argument involves distinguishing the ground or basis of love, on the one hand, and the object of love, on the other.[27] For instance, I may love my wife because she possesses certain qualities, but the object of my love is my wife, not those qualities. Although the particular states or events or properties of Mary's that Hall says John loves may be the ground or basis of John's love of Mary, still the object of his love is Mary, not some states of affairs involving Mary. After all, the abstract state of affairs of Mary's having a pair of blue eyes exists even in possible worlds in which Mary does not have blue eyes, but surely John would not love this state of affairs in those worlds.

In a related vein, Michael Zimmerman argues that whenever a person claims that some particular, concrete thing is intrinsically valuable, we can actually locate the value in question not in the thing itself, but rather in "some state of the object" in question.[28] Just as object causation can be reduced to event causation, with an accompanying increase in understanding, he argues that claims about the intrinsic value of objects can be reduced to claims about the intrinsic value of concrete states of such objects.[29] But in discussing this idea, Zimmerman considers in detail only certain kinds of examples from the literature, namely, those that are designed to show that intrinsic value might depend upon some nonintrinsic property. These include Korsgaard's examples of mink coats, fine china, and gorgeously enameled frying pans, Kagan's example of Abraham Lincoln's pen, and Rabinowicz and Rønnow-Rasmussen's example of a dress that once belonged to Princess Diana.[30] Hence Zimmerman's discussion suffers from a failure to keep these two issues distinct.

This shortcoming becomes most clear when he compares the goodness of the concrete objects mentioned earlier to the goodness of pleasure:

---

27 Brentlinger 1970.
28 Zimmerman 2001, p. 39.
29 Zimmerman 2001, pp. 39ff.
30 Zimmerman 2001, pp. 37ff.

In the case of pleasure, there was no helpful explanation why pleasure is good, and this fact fits well with the observation that the value of pleasure is nonderivative. But if we explain the values of the coat, the china, the pan, the pen, and the dress by appealing to certain relational properties of these objects rather than to their own natures, this seems to me a strong indication that these values are derivative and that we must press our inquiry further in order to reach the nonderivative values that are their sources.[31]

Zimmerman is clearly right about the way that the authors in question appeal to extrinsic properties in order to explain the value of these objects, and for this reason, I join with him in rejecting those arguments. But what would Zimmerman say to a person who found these same objects intrinsically valuable not in virtue of any relational, extrinsic properties they have, but rather in virtue of their intrinsic properties instead? Here we should reject Kagan's claim that Lincoln's pen would have had no intrinsic value at all if it did not have its peculiar history, and insist instead that it would have had the same intrinsic value as any other pen of that same type.[32]

As mentioned earlier, Zimmerman's argument gains a specious air of plausibility because he considers only cases designed to show that intrinsic value might depend upon extrinsic properties. This is because in these cases, it is easy to trace the value away from the objects themselves and toward specific states of theirs. His criticism of the Kantian view of the infinite intrinsic value of persons may be on target,[33] but there is a middle ground in between this extreme Kantian view and the view that concrete objects are not bearers of intrinsic value at all. My Main Conclusion is situated squarely within this middle ground.

Zimmerman's positive proposal that concrete states are the only bearers of intrinsic value is intriguing, given my argument

---

31 Zimmerman 2001, p. 38, emphasis in the original.
32 Kagan 1998, p. 285; for more on this, see Chapter 5.
33 See Zimmerman 2001, pp. 45–6.

developed above (by way of criticism of Lemos) to the effect that the intrinsic value that we often attribute to abstract states of affairs is actually located in concrete particular things (namely, those concrete particular things that explain why the abstract states of affairs in question obtain). Simplifying matters a bit, Zimmerman thinks of a concrete state as an ordered triple <x, P, t>, where x is an object or person, P is a property, and t is an instant of time.[34] His proposal handles nicely my complaint against Lemos by connecting intrinsic value to concrete particular objects.

But what determines the degree of the intrinsic value of a given concrete state? Zimmerman claims that in every case, the intrinsic value of a concrete state comes from its constituent property P, never from the object x or the time t.[35] For instance, in the intrinsically valuable concrete state described by <John, being deservedly pleased, t>, he claims that the property in question (namely, being deservedly pleased) is doing all of the work.

By contrast, Rabinowicz and Rønnow-Rasmussen claim that approaches like Zimmerman's put the cart before the horse, since "it is the state that derives its value from the object it involves and not the other way round."[36] Anderson evidently would agree, since she says that in general, "States of affairs which consist in the existence of something are valuable only if it makes sense to care about the thing that exists."[37]

Zimmerman and I agree that properties are doing the work with respect to intrinsic value, but we disagree about the actual bearers of intrinsic value. I regard the intrinsic possession of a property by a thing as the ground or basis of the intrinsic value of that thing, whereas Zimmerman believes that the concrete state of a thing's possessing a property at a time is intrinsically valuable (and the thing in question is not intrinsically valuable at all). Zimmerman points out correctly that the properties that a person has at a time are doing the

---

34 See Zimmerman 2001, pp. 52ff for the nonsimplified version of his account of the nature of concrete states.
35 Zimmerman 2001, p. 63.
36 Rabinowicz and Rønnow-Rasmussen 1999, p. 43.
37 Anderson 1993, p. 26 (quoted in Rabinowicz and Rønnow-Rasmussen 1999, p. 43, fn. 17).

work (and would do the same work for someone else), but this does not count against my view, according to which the possession of the relevant properties is the ground or basis of intrinsic value.

I would raise the following question for Zimmerman's view: in what sense is the property in question doing the work of explaining the intrinsic value of the concrete state, according to his view? The property is an essential ingredient in the concrete state of affairs, all right,[38] but the existence of the property all by itself explains nothing. The property is instantiated only when it is possessed by a concrete individual at a time, and only then does the question of intrinsic value arise.[39] So in what sense is the property doing the work of explaining the intrinsic value in question? It seems to me that it is the concrete individual's possession of the property that is doing the work, not the property itself.[40] Perhaps Zimmerman could distinguish the property itself, on the one hand, from its instances or tropes, on the other hand, and argue that property instances or tropes are doing all of the work.[41] This would be a step closer to my view, I think, because those very property instances or tropes are very closely tied to the individuals that possess them. (In fact, they could not be possessed by other subjects at all; but this implication would complicate Zimmerman's claim that those same properties would do the same work for another person.)

So I think that we should grant to Zimmerman that if there exists a concrete state of the form <John, being deservedly pleased, t>, then it has some degree of intrinsic value.[42] But this does not

---

38 According to Zimmerman, concrete states have all of their parts essentially: see Zimmerman 2001, pp. 54–64.
39 Presumably Zimmerman would say that the uninstantiated property of being deservedly pleased is not intrinsically valuable in any possible world.
40 Zimmerman says as much himself (Zimmerman 2001, p. 48); this point is similar to the criticism of Lemos's view that states of affairs are intrinsically valuable (see Section 1 above).
41 Fara suggests that Prior, Pargetter, and Jackson's account of dispositions would be stronger if similarly modified, because causal explanation needs to appeal to events or tropes, not just to properties: Fara 2009.
42 Incidentally, it seems that being deservedly pleased is not a property that one can possess intrinsically, given how I have defined this notion (a perfect duplicate of John would not be deservedly pleased), but I shall ignore this complication here.

preclude the possibility that John himself is also intrinsically valuable to some degree on the basis of his intrinsic structure. In fact, we have found no convincing arguments against counting concrete particular objects as bearers of intrinsic value.

3. Conclusion

Zimmerman notes that if the bearers of intrinsic value are "ontologically mixed," as my Ambitious Speculative Conclusion claims they are, then there is little hope for a formula that would enable us to compute the intrinsic value of a whole composed of parts. Then he cites this fact, together with simplicity, as advantages of his view that concrete states are the only bearers of intrinsic value.[43]

From a systematic point of view, Zimmerman is clearly right about these advantages of his view. But independently of these virtues, there are important obstacles in the way of the computation of the intrinsic value of a whole on the basis of its parts. These obstacles include the apparent incommensurability of various intrinsic values and the apparent phenomenon of organic unity.[44] We will see in Chapter 5 that there are additional reasons to regard the bearers of intrinsic value as "ontologically mixed," so if this plurality regarding intrinsic value makes computation more difficult, well, then so much the worse for computation.

In conclusion, there are no convincing arguments against counting either abstract objects or concrete particular objects as bearers of intrinsic value. This is an important part of my Main Conclusion, the view that every concrete particular thing is intrinsically valuable to some degree. Together with the discussion of abstract objects in Section 1 of this chapter, this completes the first half of my defense of the Ambitious Speculative Conclusion, the view that something in every exemplified

---

43 Zimmerman, p. 46.
44 Zimmerman himself discusses these obstacles, plus another one, in Zimmerman 2010. The desire to have an account of intrinsic value that permits the appearance of numerical computation may be a manifestation of the regrettable trend mentioned in footnote 20 of Chapter 2; see also the discussion of criteria in Chapters 5 and 6.

ontological category is intrinsically valuable to some degree. The second half of my defense of this claim will be presented in Chapter 5. But before turning to that task, I shall consider in Chapter 4 the possibility of a nonarbitrary answer to the Cutoff Question posed in Chapter 2; this should help to highlight further the theoretical advantages of my Main Conclusion as compared to its chief rivals.

4 The Cutoff Question

In the previous chapter, I argued that concrete particular things could be bearers of intrinsic value. And in Chapter 2, I briefly discussed a particular case of this when I claimed that my three children were intrinsically valuable. The intrinsic value of children is a natural belief, the sort of thing to which people appeal as a premise in moral arguments, and the sort of thing that people find bewildering to deny. This does not mean that it is true, and I have no noncircular argument that can be used to demonstrate that it is. But it seems to be confirmed by the Annihilation Test, because it seems that a fully informed, properly functioning valuer would regard the annihilation of a child as a significant loss.[1] So we have some reason to think that human beings are intrinsically valuable. But what about everything else in the world? What about nonhuman animals? What about plants? Is every other concrete particular thing intrinsically valuable to some degree also, or is there a cutoff point somewhere between human beings and other things?

In Chapter 2, I called this "The Cutoff Question." I shall begin the investigation of this question by considering the possibility that intrinsic value is limited to human beings. Then I explore various other attempts to provide nonarbitrary answers to the Cutoff Question, keeping in mind the contrary possibility (namely, my Main Conclusion) that every concrete particular thing is intrinsically valuable to some degree. Some of these authors are not really trying to answer the Cutoff Question, as I have posed it here, but instead trying to draw some other kind of morally significant distinction between different kinds of beings. Here I shall consider

---

1 See the brief discussion of Loptsor in Chapter 2, Section 3, and in Section 4 of this chapter.

their answers as answers to the Cutoff Question instead, hoping to make some progress in answering the Distribution Question. Finally, I shall argue that the failure to locate a nonarbitrary answer to the Cutoff Question, together with considerations of theoretical simplicity, provides us with a reason for embracing the Main Conclusion.

Before making this case, though, it is important to say something about the apparent resemblance between my argument in this chapter and the well-known paradox of the sorites.[2] I do this in Section 1, before turning to the Cutoff Question in the remainder of this chapter.

1. A Sorites Paradox?

Here is an example of the sorites paradox:

> P1. A pile of 1,000 stones is a heap of stones.
>
> P2. If a pile of 1,000 stones is a heap of stones, then so is a pile of 999 stones.
>
> P3. If a pile of 999 stones is a heap of stones, then so is a pile of 998 stones.
>
> . . .
>
> C. 1 stone is a heap of stones.

The sorites is paradoxical because each premise seems to be true, the argument form seems to be valid, and yet the conclusion seems to be obviously false. As Dominic Hyde explains, the key feature of the paradox seems to be the vagueness of the key predicate involved (in this case, *heap*). Because of its vagueness, the predicate "tolerates" sufficiently small changes, such as the change between n stones and n-1 stones.[3]

Someone might reconstruct my argument concerning the Cutoff Question in the form of a sorites paradox as follows:

---

[2] Thanks to Yujin Nagasawa and Phil Goggans for suggesting this. For a detailed discussion of the history of the sorites and various ways of responding to it, see Hyde 2008.

[3] This terminology is due to Wright 1975 (cited in Hyde 2008).

P1. This human being A is intrinsically valuable.

P2. If this human being A is intrinsically valuable, then this thing B, which differs from A only slightly, is intrinsically valuable, too.

P3. If this thing B is intrinsically valuable, then this thing C, which differs from B only slightly, is intrinsically valuable, too.

. . .

C. Z is intrinsically valuable (for any thing Z).

In this chapter, I do argue that there is no plausible, nonarbitrary answer to the Cutoff Question concerning intrinsic value. As the sorites paradox involving the heap shows, there is no plausible, nonarbitrary answer to the question about how many stones are needed to constitute a heap. But this does not trouble us or prevent us from using the word *heap* with success. Should we respond in this same way to our apparent inability to answer the Cutoff Question in a plausible, nonarbitrary way? Is my argument involving intrinsic value essentially the same kind of argument as the sorites paradox involving the heap?

I don't think so. There are some important differences between the key concepts involved in these two cases. The concept of being a heap is highly vague, whereas the concept of being intrinsically valuable is not highly vague.[4] (By way of reminder, something is intrinsically valuable to a certain degree if and only if its intrinsic structure would lead fully informed, properly functioning valuers to value it for its own sake to that degree.) Also, being a heap is an all-or-nothing concept (we cannot say that one pile is more of a heap than another pile), whereas being intrinsically valuable is something that varies by degrees. So we should hesitate to assume that our reaction to the sorites paradox involving the heap would be an appropriate reaction to the apparently parallel argument involving intrinsic value. In addition, the conclusion of the

---

4 Of course, not everyone would agree with me about this; see Dancy 2000 and Schroeder 2008 (including the supplement) for discussions of value holism.

argument about intrinsic value is not obviously false, so that this argument fails to satisfy the conditions for constituting a soritical series.[5] I conclude that the comparison between the sorites paradox involving the heap and the apparently parallel argument involving intrinsic value does not, all by itself, render pointless the following investigation of the Cutoff Question.[6]

More importantly, the question here is what we should expect to find, given different theories about the distribution of intrinsic value in the world. As I shall argue at the end of the Chapter, the failure to find a plausible, nonarbitrary answer to the Cutoff Question is something that we should expect to find on the assumption that my Main Conclusion is true, but not something we should expect to find on the assumption that only some things in the world are intrinsically valuable. At best, this is an overridable, comparative judgment, not a knock-down argument for my favored position.

2. Historical Anthropocentrism

There is an old philosophical tradition in the West according to which human beings alone possess a special kind of value because of their distinctive rational capacities. This tradition is clearly present in Plato and Aristotle, and it can be traced through Western philosophy down to the present day. It remains a received doctrine, despite a number of powerful challenges raised against it in the second half of the twentieth century.[7]

To choose only one influential example, Immanuel Kant argued famously that only persons deserve respect in virtue of possessing intrinsic worth.[8] Here is one of his arguments in this vein, which involves an appeal to some kind of replacement test:

---

5 See Barnes 1982 (cited in Hyde 2008).
6 Knapp draws a similar conclusion about the difference between the standard sorites argument and his criticisms of attempts to locate a nonarbitrary threshold for moral standing (see Knapp 2007, p. 190).
7 For more on this history, see White 1967 and Passmore 1975.
8 Kant scholars will point out in haste that what I am calling intrinsic value is not the same thing as what Kant calls intrinsic worth (see the discussion of this point in Zimmerman 2001, pp. 45–6 and Bradley 2006). This may be so, but Kant's view still serves as a helpful point of departure, since it is especially influential.

> In the kingdom of ends everything has either value or dignity. Whatever has a value can be replaced by something else which is equivalent; whatever, on the other hand, is above all value, and therefore admits of no equivalent, has a dignity.
>
> . . .[T]hat which constitutes the condition under which alone anything can be an end in itself, this has not merely a relative worth, that is, value, but an intrinsic worth, that is, dignity.
>
> Now morality is the condition under which alone a rational being can be an end in himself, since by this alone it is possible that he should be a legislating member in the kingdom of ends. Thus morality, and humanity as capable of it, is that which alone has dignity. . . . [F]idelity to promises, benevolence from principle (not from instinct), have an intrinsic worth. Neither nature nor art contains anything which in default of these it could put in their place, for their worth consists not in the effects which spring from them, not in the use and advantage which they secure, but in the disposition of mind, that is, the maxims of the will which are ready to manifest themselves in such actions, even though they should not have the desired effect. . . . This estimation therefore shows that the worth of such a disposition is dignity, and places it infinitely above all value, with which it cannot for a moment be brought into comparison or competition without as it were violating its sanctity.[9]

Given what we have learned about human brains and animal capacities in the last half century, Kant's argument here is no longer plausible. The ability to act for reasons (roughly, what Kant calls having "maxims of will") is a complex ability that involves the coordination of a number of simpler abilities, such as the ability to have beliefs and to form desires. As a result of brain injuries, human beings can lose some of these capacities but not others, becoming less than fully functioning persons.[10] We also know that

---

9 Kant 1949, pp. 434–5.
10 And presumably becoming less intrinsically valuable to some degree; see the discussion below. For a lively and accessible account of some of these brain injury cases, see the classic Sacks 1985.

nonhuman animals possess these abilities to varying degrees. In fact, some nonhuman animals, like chimpanzees and dolphins, appear to act for reasons that are very similar to moral reasons.[11] So it appears that Kant was wrong to insist that human beings are the only creatures with intrinsic worth or dignity. If human beings have intrinsic worth in virtue of possessing certain so-called "higher capacities," then the nonhuman animals that possess those very same capacities to a lesser degree (and the human beings that possess them to a diminished degree) must also possess intrinsic worth, although to a lesser degree. This same pattern of argument can be repeated for a large number of features thought to distinguish human beings from everything else on earth.[12]

But if human beings and other animals are intrinsically valuable to different degrees, then what about plants? What about things on the border between the living and nonliving, like viruses? What about nonliving machines and other artifacts? Is there any way to answer the Cutoff Question in a nonarbitrary manner?

In the next few sections, I shall consider a number of important contemporary attempts to draw an ethically significant, nonarbitrary cutoff point.[13] The fact that all of these attempts are failures suggests that the Cutoff Question may have no satisfactory answer at all, that perhaps everything that exists is intrinsically valuable to some degree— or so I shall argue, at the end of this chapter.

3. Adams and Egalitarianism

Robert Adams argues that there is a "complex package of features that constitutes the excellence of persons as such," and that permits

---

11 For more on this, see Rachels 1990, DeGrazia 1996, MacIntyre 1999, Varner 1998, and Agar 2001.
12 For a list of some 33 properties (that's right, 33 of them!) thought to do the job, together with a brief diagnosis as to why each one fails, see Routley and Routley 1979, pp. 109–10. A cottage industry has sprouted up around poking holes in attempts to answer versions of the Cutoff Question, but this strikes me as rather like shooting fish in a barrel, so here I shall consider only a few well-known, representative examples.
13 These are all attempts to locate what Mark Bernstein calls a "morally relevant property" (see Bernstein 2002, pp. 531ff.).

us both (1) to justify the claim that human beings are distinctive and (2) to ground the moral claim of the equality of all persons:

> What distinguishes us from dogs and daisies is a complex system of features reasonably regarded as excellent. It includes rationality, but also emotional, social, and creative capacities related to rationality but going beyond it in various ways.[14]

What is especially interesting about the first claim, which is an attempt to answer the Cutoff Question, is that Adams recognizes explicitly that those properties that seem to make human beings distinctively good are properties that vary by degrees among humans and are also possessed to some degree by other animals.[15]

How does Adams argue for the conclusion that the complex package of features that constitutes the excellence of persons can ground some kind of moral egalitarianism among human beings? He argues that this complex package does not permit rankings of relative excellence between persons for two reasons. First, he argues that since excellence is multidimensional, it is "not an intensive magnitude that can be completely and consistently ordered on a scale of value."[16] By way of example, he mentions the absurdity of trying to decide which chimpanzee in a group of chimpanzees is most like a human being, citing a variety of obstacles that would prevent us from arriving at a single, clearly correct answer. He says that

> We may reasonably believe that human persons are globally more like God than sheep are, while resisting any attempt to rank individual persons on their global resemblance to God, since so many dimensions of comparison are relevant, and the resemblance is so distant, though still of the greatest importance.[17]

---

14 Adams 1999, p. 117; the arguments discussed in the following paragraphs occur on pp. 115–21. For a discussion of the relation between Adams's notion of excellence and my notion of intrinsic value, see Chapter 7, Section 1 below.
15 Adams 1999, p. 117.
16 Adams 1999, p. 117.
17 Adams 1999, p. 117.

The multidimensional nature of human excellence makes it a richer resemblance to God than one based on any single property alone (such as rationality), and grounds a "qualitative superiority" of the excellence of persons as such, as opposed to the "much narrower excellences with regard to which we can clearly excel each other."[18] Second, Adams argues that this excellence is not additive in the sense that more of it is not necessarily better.[19]

We can grant to Adams that his complex package of features would not enable us to provide a complete ranking of all human persons relative to one another in terms of relative excellence. But this does not mean that there are no clear cases of difference between persons relative to this complex package of features. Adams's use of the word *globally* in the longer quotation cited above is revealing: he seems to be arguing that human persons *as a group* are distinctive, not that every individual human being is more excellent than any other nonhuman animal. In other words, Adams simply ignores here those borderline cases in which (i) some nonhuman animals possess a high degree of those properties that contribute to human excellence and those borderline cases in which (ii) some human beings possess those same properties only to a small degree (if at all). For this reason, his account of human excellence cannot be viewed as providing a satisfactory answer to the Cutoff Question.

4. Life

Tom Regan claims that all experiencing subjects of a life are inherently valuable to the same degree, and nothing else is.[20] Since he contends that inherent value must be an all-or-nothing affair, I chose to discuss his argument in an earlier chapter (Chapter 2, Section 2). The problem with Regan's argument here is that being a subject of a life is a matter of possessing a number of other properties, the possession of which varies by degrees and fades from

---

18   Adams 1999, p. 118.
19   Adams 1999, p. 118–19.
20   As noted in Chapter 2, Regan's notion of inherent value is broader than my notion of intrinsic value, but includes something like intrinsic value as a subcomponent.

clear affirmative cases (such as fully functioning human beings) to borderline cases (such as simple mammals) to clear negative cases (such as insects).

If we depart from Regan by recognizing degrees of intrinsic value among living things, as it seems we should, then it seems quite arbitrary to restrict intrinsic value to living things alone. Kenneth Goodpaster disagrees. He argues that being alive is a minimal condition on moral considerability.[21] After moving away from a human-centered theory of moral considerability, he stops short at the boundary between the living and the nonliving:

> Neither rationality nor the capacity to experience pleasure and pain seem to me to be necessary (even though they may be sufficient) conditions on moral considerability. And only our hedonistic and concentric forms of ethical reflection keep us from acknowledging this fact. Nothing short of the condition of being alive seems to me to be a plausible and nonarbitrary criterion.[22]

But why is being alive so important? What is it about living things that distinguishes them from everything else? Perhaps some help here comes from Paul W. Taylor, who argues that something possesses inherent worth just in case

> Its good is deserving of the concern and consideration of all moral agents, and the realization of its good has intrinsic value, to be pursued as an end in itself and for the sake of the entity whose good it is.[23]

According to Taylor, for each and every living thing, there is a good for that thing, a way of benefiting or harming it.

---

[21] Again, this is not the same concept as the concept of intrinsic value, but it is still helpful to consider his argument as providing a nonarbitrary answer to the Cutoff Question.
[22] Goodpaster 1978.
[23] Taylor 1981, pp. 197–218; see also von Wright 1963.

But aren't there complicated nonliving things, like computers and other machines, that can properly be said to have goods of their own?[24] After all, we regularly speak about the good of machines: riding the clutch is not good for the car, letting the lawn mower run out of oil is bad for it, static electricity is not good for the computer, and so on. By way of reply, Goodpaster could argue that the goods of the machines in question are really just goods for human beings, not the goods of the machines themselves. As it happens, Nicholas Agar argues in just this way:

> The goal of the thermostat is maintenance of a human friendly temperature, and this is its good; so the widespread destruction of thermostats will generate moral wrong only if other devices capable of maintaining temperature for us are not installed.[25]

Agar contrasts the goal of the thermostat with the goals of living things, which have "biopreferences" that are selected over many generations, according to his representational theory of life, giving them goals of their own, so to speak.[26]

It must be admitted that Agar makes a reasonable point. When we say that something is good for a machine, typically we mean that it is instrumentally good in the sense that it enhances its function for us.[27] So riding the clutch can make the car dangerous to its passengers, letting the lawn mower run out of oil can make the engine stop working, and static electricity can cause damage to the data stored on one's computer. In all of these cases, what is said to be good for the machine in question is really just good for

---

24 Taylor himself leaves this question open, and hence does not consider whether nonliving things might have intrinsic value.
25 Agar 2001, p. 100. Hereafter, page citations to Agar's work refer to this publication, unless otherwise indicated.
26 See Agar, pp. 92ff.
27 I say "typically" here, because sometimes when we speak about what is good or bad for a thing, we are also talking simply about what is necessary for it to exist, whether or not it also serves our purposes. See the discussion of this point in connection with Sober's argument in Chapter 6, Section 1.

the humans who use it, so that what we are really talking about here is instrumental value, not intrinsic value.

But is that the end of the matter? To return to Agar's example of the thermostats, is it really true that the widespread destruction of thermostats would involve no loss of intrinsic value? Let's apply the Annihilation Test. Would a fully informed, properly functioning valuer regard the annihilation of an ordinary thermostat as a loss?

This is an important point, and one that some have found puzzling, so let me explain it as carefully as I can. Since the outcome of this argument can be generalized to cover any concrete particular thing, in what follows I shall refer to it as the "Anything is Better than Nothing" argument.[28]

Compare the following two scenarios: in one, our fully informed, properly functioning valuer witnesses the annihilation of a thermostat: the thermostat is placed in the machine, the button is pressed, and it disappears. In the second scenario, our fully informed, properly functioning valuer witnesses the annihilation of nothing: the machine is empty, but the button is pressed anyway, resulting in no change at all. Our fully informed, properly functioning valuer will be indifferent to the activation of the machine in the second scenario, since it involves no change, but what about the first scenario? The first scenario involves a change, however slight: an intrinsic structure is missing from the world.[29] It would be a mistake to be completely indifferent to this change, to respond to it in the same way as if nothing had happened at all; this would indicate a failure to track a change in the world, however slight. And this is just what one would expect if the Main Conclusion is true, since it claims that all concrete particular things are intrinsically valuable to some degree.

Of course, to return to the question of machines, there are degrees of complexity and functional organization to consider here.

---

28 For a discussion of arguments purporting to show that some concrete particular things are intrinsically bad, see Chapter 5, Section 3.
29 Thanks to Xu Yingjin for many suggestions concerning how to describe the change that the valuer would recognize in this case.

When compared to the intrinsic structure of a mouse, for instance, the intrinsic structure of a thermostat is singularly unimpressive. But some living things are rather simple and some machines are rather impressive.[30] Goodpaster's suggestion also faces the problem of trying to draw a nonarbitrary distinction between living and nonliving things. (This is a significant philosophical question, and one that I am happy to leave to others to address.) If all living things deserve some degree of moral considerability, as he claims they do, regardless of their complexity and functional organization, then it seems quite arbitrary to deny the same to machines of comparable structure. Hence Goodpaster's suggested answer to the Cutoff Question fails as well.

5. Singer on Sentience

A different possibility is suggested by the following well-known argument from Peter Singer, who says that with respect to the idea of having interests,[31] the line should be drawn at sentience, the capacity to feel pleasure or pain:

> By saying that we must consider the interests of all beings with the capacity for suffering or enjoyment, Bentham does not arbitrarily exclude from consideration any interests at all—as those who draw the line with reference to the possession of reason or language do. The capacity for suffering and enjoyment is a prerequisite for having interests at all, a condition that must be satisfied before we can speak of interests in a meaningful way. It would be nonsense to say that it was not in the interests of a stone to be kicked along the road by a schoolboy. A stone does not have interests because it cannot suffer. Nothing that we can do to it could possibly make any

---

30 Mark Murphy has reminded me (in correspondence) me that having a function and being a machine are extrinsic properties of things. This is so, but machines have intrinsic structures that explain the dispositions that enable them to do what they do, and it is those intrinsic structures, strictly speaking, that ground their intrinsic value. See Chapter 5, Section 2.

31 Which is quite different from the idea of having intrinsic value, of course; Singer is not trying to answer our Cutoff Question here, but rather a different one.

difference to its welfare. A mouse, on the other hand, does have an interest in not being kicked along the road, because it will suffer if it is.[32]

Agar agrees with Singer about the stone, although for different reasons: it has no "content-characterizable goals," no "structure whose biofunction is to produce movement or change":

> In pushing a boulder down a hill, we interfere with no goal, and therefore no good, of the boulder. Stepping on a cockroach approaching a food scrap is a quite different matter. The cockroach possesses environment-directed internal states whose biofunction is to enable it to retrieve the food scraps.[33]

These arguments are simply not persuasive when considered in terms of intrinsic value. Of course, the notion of having interests (or biofunctions) is not the same as the notion of having intrinsic value. The stone in question certainly does not have interests in the usual sense, and this is an important difference between the mouse and the stone. No respectable theory of degrees of intrinsic value should imply anything to the contrary. But it does not follow from any of this that the stone has no intrinsic value at all.[34]

In order to see that this is so, let's return to the Anything is Better than Nothing argument and consider the different ways in which a thing might be destroyed. If the stone were destroyed by being broken into two pieces by a hammer, then we might think that no intrinsic value had been lost in the world, since we might think of the resulting stones as being essentially just like the original stone, although smaller in size.[35] Similar things might be said about many other kinds of objects, where dividing them results in

---

[32] Singer 1981, p. 199.
[33] Agar, pp. 93, 95.
[34] Just to be clear, only Agar draws this conclusion about the stone; as noted earlier, Singer is not talking about intrinsic value in the passage quoted above.
[35] We do not typically think that being larger implies being more intrinsically valuable; this is one of the important lessons to be drawn from the sobering tale in Seuss 1954.

creating more of the same kind of thing. A fully informed, properly functioning valuer who tracked the change in the world brought about by the division of the stone would need to consider not just the destruction of the original stone, but also the creation of the two new ones.

But things would be different if the stone were annihilated instead of split in two—something of intrinsic value would have been lost from the world. It might be a very tiny degree of intrinsic value, to be sure, especially when compared to the intrinsic value of a typical human being or a dog or a mouse, but it would be missing nonetheless. A fully informed, properly functioning valuer would not be completely indifferent to the annihilation of the stone, as if nothing at all had happened. Hence it seems to me that any attempt to answer the Cutoff Question based upon Singer's approach is bound to fail as well.

At this point, some readers might worry about my thought experiments involving the Annihilation Test for the following reason: what if we had a creation machine that worked just like the annihilation machine, but in reverse? What if pushing the button on the creation machine resulted in creating something out of nothing? How would the fully informed, properly functioning valuer respond to that? And if the fully informed, properly functioning valuer would respond favorably, doesn't it follow that we are obligated to create more things of intrinsic value in the world, perhaps by splitting rocks and cutting our noodles and dividing sticks of butter wherever possible?

Given what I have said about intrinsic structures and duplicates,[36] it does follow that a fully informed, properly functioning valuer would respond favorably to the creation of a new thing, any thing. This means that such a thing, any thing, would have some degree of intrinsic value. But I do not argue or assume in this book that we are obligated to maximize the intrinsic value in the world.[37] Also, there is a fundamental asymmetry between duties or obligations

---

36 See Chapter 1, Section 2.
37 Adams (1999, p. 119) argues that beyond a certain threshold, more of a certain thing does not necessarily make a world better. For more on ethics and intrinsic value, see Chapter 6.

to create things, on the one hand, and duties or obligations not to destroy existing things, on the other hand; the latter are much more stringent and demanding than the former. So the possibility of a creation machine poses no difficulty for my arguments here.

5. Conclusion

Although I have not surveyed every possible answer to the Cutoff Question here, the theme that is emerging is that there is no plausible, nonarbitrary way to answer it that is more plausible than the Main Conclusion sketched in Chapter 3, according to which all existing things enjoy some degree of intrinsic value, however small. The argument of this Chapter is a clear case of what Gary Gutting calls a "Challenge Argument," where failed attempts to meet a certain challenge over a long period of time start to provide evidence that the challenge simply cannot be met.[38]

Consider again Figure 3:

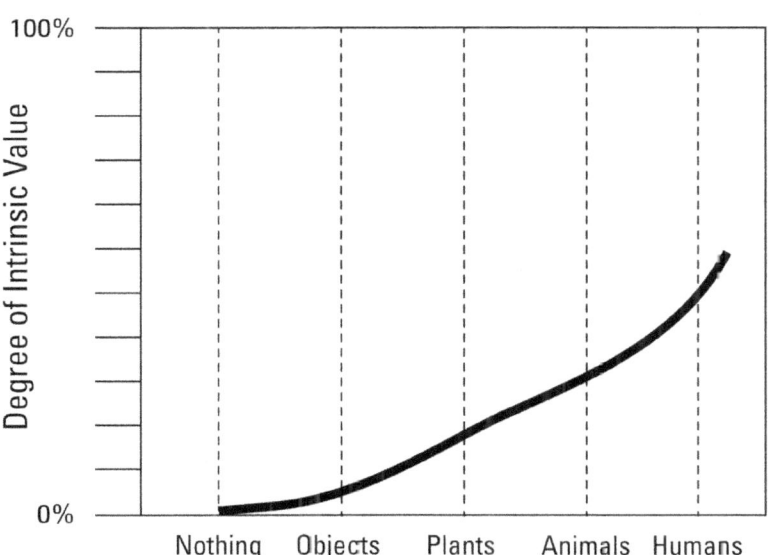

Figure 3 The Possibility of Ubiquitous Intrinsic Value Varying by Degrees

---

38 Gutting 2009, pp. 73ff. Those who are interested in other attempts to answer some form of the Cutoff Question should start by reading Routley and Routley 1979.

76 On the Intrinsic Value of Everything

This figure, which represents my Main Conclusion, clearly requires no answer to the Cutoff Question, since it depicts intrinsic value as fading to nothing as it approaches nonexistence, so to speak.[39] Now compare Figure 3 to Figure 5, which represents the next most plausible picture of degrees of intrinsic value described in Chapter 2, and which clearly presupposes some answer to the Cutoff Question:

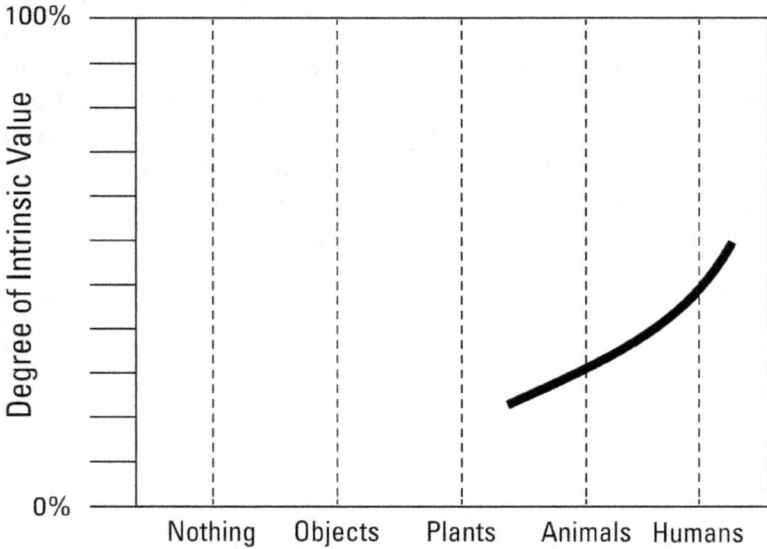

Figure 5 The Possibility of Restricted Intrinsic Value Varying By Degrees

The picture depicted in Figure 3 is theoretically simpler than the one depicted in Figure 5. The distribution of intrinsic value depicted in Figure 5 cries out for a nonarbitrary answer to the Cutoff Question: why does it end there? What distinguishes things

---

39 This is not drawn to scale—the exact shape of the curved part of the line in Figure 3 (and also in Figure 5) is arbitrary; I am not committed to the precise proportions here (see the discussion of this question in Chapter 5, Section 2 below). See Chapter 7 for an elaboration of Figure 3 to include God, which results in a symmetric termination of the line at the top of the scale of possible degrees of intrinsic value.

that have intrinsic value to some degree from those that lack it altogether? What intrinsic structure is possessed by things marked by the line, and not possessed by things not marked by the line? If things were really like this, we would expect to be able to answer the Cutoff Question in a plausible, nonarbitrary way.

Of course, Figure 1 from Chapter 2 (representing The Possibility of Complete Intrinsic Value Neutrality, or the view that nothing at all is intrinsically valuable) is theoretically simpler than either Figure 3 or Figure 5:

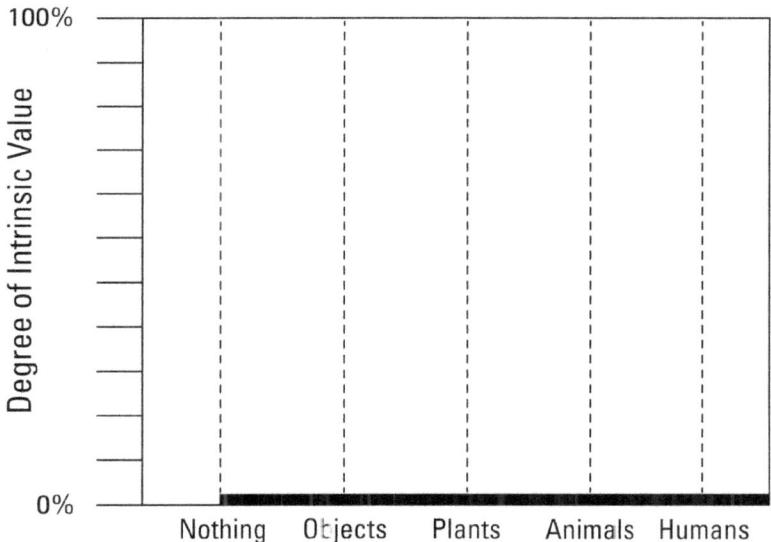

Figure 1 The Possibility of Complete Intrinsic Value Neutrality

I cannot prove in a noncircular way that this view is false, but it is incompatible with the commonsense beliefs about the intrinsic value of children mentioned at the beginning of this Chapter and the results of the Annihilation Test. So I conclude that considerations of theoretical simplicity, together with these additional considerations, tilt the scales in favor of the view depicted in Figure 3 (i.e. my Main Conclusion) over the views depicted in Figures 5 and 1.

In Chapter 1, I said that determining the ontological seriousness of my Main Conclusion would involve making difficult holistic judgments, and this is surely one of them. Since providing a plausible account of degrees of intrinsic value should help to clarify some of the issues involved in this complex comparative judgment, I shall devote the next chapter to that task.

5 Degrees

In Chapter 4, I argued that there are no good prospects for providing a plausible, nonarbitrary answer to the Cutoff Question. I also argued that a number of considerations provide us with some reason for thinking that the Main Conclusion is true: considerations of theoretical simplicity, a natural belief about the intrinsic value of children, and the results of the Annihilation Test. In this chapter, I develop an account of degrees of intrinsic value in order to complete my case for this conclusion, the view that every concrete particular thing is intrinsically valuable to some degree. I shall also add to my argument for the Ambitious Speculative Conclusion, the view that something from every exemplified ontological category is intrinsically valuable to some degree.

1. Intrinsic Value and Natures

Let's begin with an ancient debate among the pre-Socratic Milesian philosophers.[1] Thales claimed that everything in the world was composed of water in various states. One of his younger associates, Anaximander, believed that Thales's view could not account for the presence of true opposites in nature, those substances that cannot coexist in the same place at the same time, such as fire and water. So he suggested instead that the underlying substance of which all things are composed must not have any specific features at all, let alone the features specific to either one of a pair of opposites like fire and water. He named this underlying stuff "the indifferent."

One of Anaximander's students, Anaximenes, rejected this approach entirely, suggesting instead that the underlying substance

---

1 In what follows, I am summarizing a familiar way of understanding the development of philosophical thought in this period. See Jordan 1987, chapter 1, for a helpful introduction to these issues.

of the world was air (in various states of condensation and rarefaction). His argument against Anaximander involved the plausible claim that in order to exist at all, something must have a specific nature of some kind:

> To be a thing at all is to have characteristics that make it something in particular and different in certain respects from other things. A "thing without characteristics" is a contradiction in terms. The force of this point is clear from Anaximander's own failure, hard as he may have tried, to be strictly indefinite about the Indefinite. In fact he attributed to it, directly or by implication, a number of characteristics.[2]

A few centuries later, St. Augustine would argue for a related position in order to support his belief that every good thing is from God:

> Any nature you come across is from God. So if you see anything at all that has measure, number, and order, do not hesitate to attribute it to God as craftsman. If you take away all measure, number, and order, there is absolutely nothing left. . . . So if you take away everything that is good, you will have absolutely nothing left.[3]

According to St. Augustine, it is better to exist than not to exist, since existence always involves some goodness (and nonexistence cannot involve any goodness at all).

A few centuries later still, St. Thomas Aquinas would accept a version of St. Augustine's view of the relationship between existence and goodness, although he differed from his predecessors in trying to combine the Aristotelian idea of intrinsic goodness with the Platonic idea of goodness by participation.[4] According to St. Thomas, every individual substance that exists has a substantial

---

[2] This is Jordan's summary (Jordan 1987, p. 11).
[3] St. Augustine 1993, p. 69.
[4] Perhaps unsuccessfully—see the discussions in Kretzmann 1991A, MacDonald 1991B and C, and Artsen 1991.

form, which is specified by its definition, and includes a specific set of potencies or powers. A good thing of a kind X is one that actualizes fully the potencies or powers distinctive of Xs.[5] Based on this kind of approach, one might develop an account of degrees of intrinsic value for individual substances.[6]

Such an approach seems promising for concrete "perfectibles," but it faces some serious obstacles in terms of providing a complete account of degrees of intrinsic value. First, the account seems to presuppose the existence of objective, natural kinds of things, and some will regard this a bit of "outmoded and untenable essentialist metaphysics."[7] Second, the account would need to be extended to apply also to concrete imperfectibles, such as fundamental particles, which appear not to be different from one another with regard to the properties that they possess intrinsically.[8] It also does not seem to apply in any straightforward way to abstract objects, accidents of substances, or concrete events. Can the basic idea behind this account be modified to meet these challenges? Let's consider the case of concrete particular objects first. and then turn to the other kinds of things.

2. Intrinsic Value and Intrinsic Structures

For inspiration, let's return to the simple point made by Anaximander and St. Augustine: every existing thing possesses some specific properties intrinsically; there are no bare particulars, we might say (let alone bare universals!). Now some intrinsic

---

5 Here I am following the description of St. Thomas provided in Stump and Kretzmann 1991.
6 See Walhout 1978, pp. 180ff and Murphy 2001, pp. 95ff, 190ff for accounts of degrees of perfection along these lines. For an extension of Murphy's account of practical reason to include the goods of nonhuman objects as reasons for human action, see Davison 2008.
7 As is in fact Nicholas Rescher complains about Robert Hartman's theory: see Hartman 1967 and the criticism in Rescher 1982, p. 59.
8 A promising line of inquiry here might involve St. Thomas's idea that angels are individuated by their intellectual capacities—since they are immaterial beings, they cannot be individuated by matter, hence there can be only one angel per species. See the helpful discussion of St. Thomas in Pini 2012, pp. 5–18; for more on different approaches to the individuation of particulars in the middle ages, see the essays in Gracia 1994 and King 2000.

structures are intrinsically better than others: they would provide fully informed, properly functioning valuers with stronger reasons to value something for its own sake than other intrinsic structures would. How does this work, though? And what if something possesses some properties intrinsically that contribute to its intrinsic value, but also possesses other properties intrinsically, properties that detract from its intrinsic value? How would a fully informed, properly functioning valuer integrate these facts into a unified judgment concerning the thing as a whole?[9]

Some authors suggest that certain intrinsic structures are intrinsically better than others, and this is a brute, unexplained fact.[10] Although I have no sharp criteria to offer that would enable us to rank all possible intrinsic structures with respect to intrinsic value, I think we can do better than this.

First, there are some clear cases in which the intrinsic possession of a certain property makes its bearer more intrinsically valuable than it would be otherwise. The man who mistook his wife for a hat, for instance, was certainly intrinsically better before the brain injury that led him to make this mistake.[11] More generally, it seems that some animals are more intrinsically valuable than other animals, animals are more intrinsically valuable than plants, and plants are more intrinsically valuable than inanimate objects like rocks. But even rocks have a place in this scheme. If my Main Conclusion is right, then every grain of sand, every fundamental particle everywhere in the universe, every existing concrete thing has some degree of intrinsic value, no matter how small or large it is.

Here is another example of a clear difference in degrees of intrinsic value. My son has a toy plastic fish that looks very lifelike, and we should think that it has some small degree of intrinsic value. But there also exists in the museum a stuffed fish that looks just like my son's toy fish. This stuffed fish in the museum was

---

9 This problem is noted in Rabinowicz and Rønnow-Rasmussen 2004, p. 418, fn. 76.
10 See Nozick 1981, chapter 5, especially pp. 444–5. In Chapter 7, I shall also discuss the account offered by Robert Adams, according to which excellence involves some form of divine resemblance.
11 This refers to an actual case described in Sacks 1985.

once alive but is now dead, despite being very lifelike in appearance. Such a fish is more intrinsically valuable than my son's plastic fish, because of its intrinsic structure.[12] Finally, there exist many living fish in the world that look just like my son's toy plastic fish and the stuffed fish, but are more intrinsically valuable than both of those things because of their intrinsic structures.

What explains these comparative judgments concerning intrinsic value? What is the underlying pattern here? In these next few paragraphs, I shall venture an explanation, but it is important to realize that I am not trying to reduce intrinsic value to natural properties here. Instead, I am offering an explanation as to why the clear comparative judgments just described are correct, assuming that they are correct. Also, my account will apply only to concrete particular things; I shall discuss degrees of intrinsic value in other ontological categories in Section 4.

Consider a simple lump of coal. Its intrinsic structure includes what we might call its basic intrinsic properties, including its mass, shape, chemical composition, etc. This intrinsic structure explains the dispositions it has to interact with its environment, those dispositions that enable us to distinguish it from other lumps of coal and lumps of other kinds of stuff.[13]

Now consider an archaeon, which is a simple, single-celled living organism. Like the lump of coal, the archaeon's intrinsic structure includes its basic intrinsic properties, including its mass, shape, and chemical composition. But it also includes other properties that the lump of coal lacks—it has interesting, complicated structures that enable it to interact with its environment in highly selective ways. This intrinsic structure explains those distinctive dispositions in virtue of which we classify it as a living organism (namely, nutrition, growth, and decay, to use Aristotelian

---

12 I have not argued that in general, the more complex a thing is, the more intrinsically valuable it is. It seems to me that this judgment must be made on a case-by-case basis, since sometimes complexity alone does not make one thing intrinsically better than another.

13 How exactly this intrinsic structure explains these dispositions is a complicated matter: for a map of the possibilities here, see Fara 2009.

terminology). This explains why the archaeon is more intrinsically valuable than the lump of coal.

Consider now one of the rabbits that lives in my back yard. Like the archaeon, the rabbit's intrinsic structure includes its basic intrinsic properties, including its mass, shape, and chemical composition. Also like the archaeon, the rabbit has interesting, complicated structures that enable it to interact with its environment in highly selective ways—the rabbit is alive too. But the rabbit's intrinsic structure includes other properties that the archaeon's lacks—it has perception, movement, memory, etc. This intrinsic structure explains those distinctive dispositions in virtue of which we classify the rabbit as an animal, and this explains why the rabbit is more intrinsically valuable than the archaeon.

Finally, consider my 5 year old daughter, Grace. She is more intrinsically valuable than the rabbit because her intrinsic structure is richer than the rabbit's—she has rationality, self-awareness, and so on. By now, the general pattern of this account has become clear: X is more intrinsically valuable than Y because X's intrinsic structure includes all of the same types of intrinsic properties that are parts of Y's intrinsic structure, plus other, more interesting ones. This account of degrees of intrinsic value enables us to see why the clear comparative judgments described above are correct (assuming that they are correct).

But some important qualifications suggest themselves immediately. We should not assume that human beings are the most intrinsically valuable things in the universe; we must be careful to resist anthropocentrism. Here my approach differs sharply from Agar's, which arbitrarily explains degrees of intrinsic value in terms of similarity to human psychological states.[14] Intrinsic value should not be a matter of luck in this way. We might discover some day that dolphins or aliens or tiny creatures or vast objects or immaterial beings are more intrinsically valuable than

---

14 This is good news for creatures like the longnosed elephant fish, whose complex representational states are not very similar to ours, as Agar points out: see Agar, p. 96.

we are.[15] The degree of intrinsic value that a thing possesses is an objective matter to be discovered, not something that we confer upon it by fiat. As we learn more about the intrinsic structures of things, our estimations concerning their intrinsic value can be expected to change, too. We can have both false positive and false negative experiences of intrinsic value.[16] We might mistake a collection of blankets for a person, for instance, or we might discover that certain plants and animals have much more complicated and interesting lives than we expected.

Another complication here concerns the possibility of organic unities, in which the intrinsic value of the whole is greater than the sum of the intrinsic values of the parts.[17] A human being, for instance, is more intrinsically valuable than the sum of the intrinsic values of his or her parts. Agar introduces an interesting thought experiment along these lines: if we transplanted neurons from your brain into the brains other people one at a time, and we continued to do this until you had no brain left, what would happen to your intrinsic value? Agar claims that your intrinsic value would not be divided and distributed into the many recipients of your neurons, but instead that "the value of the original person would be utterly destroyed."[18] Although I disagree with the details of this argument,[19] it provides a nice illustration of organic unity: the intrinsic value of your brain is greater than the sum of the intrinsic values of its many component parts.

The possibility of organic unities generates additional complications because we may not know how all things are related to

---

15 See the discussion of God in Chapter 7 for an example of an immaterial being who would be more intrinsically valuable than anything else.
16 The possibility of this kind of error is a necessary element in any epistemologically serious account of intrinsic value (see Chapter 1, Section 4).
17 For more on this concept, see Moore 1903, p. 96, Ross 1930, p. 72, Nozick 1981, chapter 5, Chisholm 1986, chapter 7, Lemos 1994, chapters 3 and 4, and Zimmerman 2001, chapter 5. Swinburne appeals to the possibility of organic unities in order to argue that it is impossible to provide a complete list of the intrinsically valuable things in the world: see Swinburne 1998, p. 50.
18 Agar, p. 136.
19 On my view, as long as the rest of your body survives this procedure somehow, it still has some degree of intrinsic value, even if it has no brain.

each other. Given the connections between fundamental particles currently posited by physicists, for instance, it might turn out that the universe as a whole is itself a single thing of great intrinsic value.[20] Even a cursory glance at the history of science suggests that stranger possibilities yet might be discovered by future generations, possibilities that we are simply unable to foresee at the present time. So our judgments about the intrinsic values of things must always remain subject to future revision, depending as they do upon our incomplete knowledge of the existence and intrinsic structures of things.

3. Intrinsically Bad Things?

Students of the history of philosophy will recognize in the Main Conclusion an echo of the medieval doctrine that being and goodness are convertible. They might also wonder if the Main Conclusion faces similar problems, especially concerning things that appear to be intrinsically bad.[21] Does the Main Conclusion imply that nothing is bad, or that nothing that exists can be intrinsically bad?

Nicholas Rescher criticizes Robert Hartman's theory of intrinsic value for appealing to the essences of good things like saints and medicines, but ignoring the essences of bad things like sinners and poisons.[22] In a different but related vein, John O'Neill claims that

> [T]here are some entities whose flourishing simply should not enter into any [utilitarian] calculations—the flourishing of dictatorships and viruses for example. It is not the case that the goods of viruses should count, even just a very small

---

20 For an ancient view along these lines, see Plato's dialogue *Timaeus*; for more on the intrinsic value of the universe as a whole, see the discussion of Everitt's argument against the existence of God based on the scale of the universe in Chapter 7.
21 See the helpful collection of essays edited by Scott MacDonald (MacDonald 1991A) and Walhout 1978, pp. 187ff for more on the historical development and contemporary refinements of the convertibility thesis. For an engaging discussion of the Thomistic tradition focused on the work of Francisco Suarez and his treatment of things that seem to be evil *per se*, see Gracia 1991.
22 Rescher 1982, p. 59.

amount. There is no reason why these goods should count at all as ends in themselves.... The flourishing of such entities is itself a direct object of ethical appraisal.[23]

Bernstein would seem to agree with O'Neill here, noting that given typical definitions of *intrinsic value*, something that is intrinsically valuable might not be good for us to possess at all (or even positively bad for us).[24]

Here Rescher, O'Neill, and Bernstein seem to be judging the intrinsic values of various things (sinners, poisons, viruses, dictatorships, etc.) by reference to their typical effects on (other) human beings. But clearly this approach confuses intrinsic value with instrumental value (for human beings). In the same way that the Annihilation Test can be applied to a thermostat or a rock (see Chapter 4), it seems that annihilating a virus or a portion of poison would result in a loss of intrinsic value, however small; after all, anything is better than nothing.[25] Rescher's case of sinners and O'Neill's case of dictatorships are problematic for different reasons, since one cannot have a sinner without having a person and one cannot have a dictatorship without having a government. Since persons can become sinners and governments can become dictatorships, being a sinner or being a dictatorship is a property or attribute of persons or governments, respectively, not an existing thing in its own right.

In other words, as the medieval philosopher/theologians often pointed out in response to the problem of evil, no concrete

---

23 O'Neill 1992, p. 117.
24 Bernstein 2001, p. 340. Bernstein has in mind here Moore's sense of "intrinsically valuable," which depends only on a thing's intrinsic properties, and concludes that this is not a kind of value "worth the name." Galactus, whom the Silver Surfer once served as an intergalactic herald, would be an example of an intrinsically valuable (although apparently morally evil) alien person who could be very bad for us (since he consumes planets): see Lee 1966.
25 It is worth noting here that even Agar supposes that the virus T4 has a miniscule amount of intrinsic value, presumably in virtue of possessing a minimal biofunction (Agar, p. 97) although he thinks that this is too small for humans to consider all by itself in their actions or calculations.

particular things are intrinsically evil, even if they typically have bad effects on human beings. For example:

> It may be bad for me that a lion should eat me. But, [St. Thomas] Aquinas maintains, even as an injured man (the victim of evil suffered) I still succeed in being human. And the lion that eats me (the cause of the evil I suffer) is doing just what we expect a lion to do.[26]

Perhaps this is just what we should expect, given the account of degrees of intrinsic value developed above in Section 2. That account enables us to offer the following conjecture about why no concrete particular thing could ever be intrinsically bad: perhaps there is no combination of higher order properties that (1) could be possessed intrinsically by a concrete particular thing, (2) would be intrinsically bad to possess, and (3) would outweigh all of the lower order, good properties that any concrete particular thing possesses. The worst kind of malice, for instance, requires intentionality, will, and memory, all of which are plausibly regarded as contributing to one's intrinsic value. As St. Augustine would say, if we take away everything good, then nothing at all remains.[27]

But what about certain states of affairs or states of concrete objects, like a given person's experiencing pain? Aren't some of them clearly intrinsically bad? Here I shall leave behind the Main Conclusion for a while and turn to the second half of my defense of the Ambitious Speculative Conclusion.

4. Ambition and Abstracta

By way of reminder, the Ambitious Speculative Conclusion is the view that something in every exemplified ontological category is intrinsically valuable to some degree. But this statement requires

---

26 Brian Davies, in the introduction to Aquinas 2003, p. 22. "If you take away everything that is good, you will have absolutely nothing left" (St. Augustine 1993, p. 69). "And so I say that evil is not an entity, but the subject that evil befalls is, since evil is only the privation of a particular good. For example, blindness is not an entity, but the subject that blindness befalls is" (Aquinas 2003, question I, article 1 *respondeo*).

27 St. Augustine 1993, p. 69.

some clarification. There are many ways of trying to describe the different ontological categories that might be exemplified in the world. Sadly, I do not have the time or space to consider every possible kind of thing in detail here; there are just too many of them.[28] Instead, I will defend here a restricted version of this conclusion, and then explain how the argument might be extended to cover other ontological categories.

So far in this book, I have discussed in some detail the following kinds of things: (1) concrete particular objects (the subjects of my Main Conclusion, and Anderson and Adams's preferred bearers of intrinsic value); (2) concrete states of particular objects (Zimmerman and Tännsjö's preferred bearers of intrinsic value); (3) abstract states of affairs (Chisholm and Lemos's preferred bearers of intrinsic value); and (4) other abstract objects such as numbers, sets, properties, and propositions. The restricted version of the Ambitious Speculative Conclusion that I shall defend here states that if one of these ontological types (1)-(4) is exemplified, then at least one member of that type is intrinsically valuable to some degree.

In Chapter 3, we encountered a number of reasons for thinking that bearers of intrinsic value could be found of types (1), (2), and (3). I argued in that chapter that there were no good arguments against the view that bearers of intrinsic value might exist in all of these ontological categories at once. In what remains of this chapter, I shall discuss types (2), (3), and (4) in more detail, but in reverse order.

Let's begin with type (4) entities, including numbers, sets, properties, and propositions. Like everything that exists, they all possess specific properties intrinsically that distinguish them from other abstract entities of the same kind.[29] (After all, if they did not possess such distinctive properties, then what would individuate

---

28 For helpful discussions of different types of ontological categories, see Hoffman and Rosenkrantz 1994, Lowe 2006, and the helpful survey of various approaches outlined in Thomasson 2010.
29 Here I am appealing to our intuitive notion of a property possessed intrinsically, of course, since the duplication explanation introduced in Chapter 1 cannot be applied to abstract objects in a straightforward way.

them from other members of the same kind?) These distinctive properties are their intrinsic structures.

But why would anyone think that these abstract entities have any intrinsic value at all? It is certainly strange to think of such things as intrinsically valuable, for a number of reasons. First, they aren't the typical objects of our basic evaluative attitudes.[30] Second, they can't be preserved or protected, since they can't be harmed or helped. Third, they seem to be completely causally inert, and hence make no practical difference to the things we care about in the world.[31]

By now, though, we should be wary of making assumptions about what can and cannot be a bearer of intrinsic value. Let's consider more carefully the three reasons. First, just because something is not the typical object of our basic evaluative attitudes, it does not follow that it cannot be intrinsically valuable; our attitudes do not set the boundaries of the intrinsically valuable. Second, just because something cannot be preserved or protected, harmed or helped, it does not follow that it cannot be intrinsically valuable. Granted, those things that we typically think of when we imagine the bearers of intrinsic value are not like this, but that's really beside the point. Third, the fact that something is completely causally inert might imply that we can ignore it completely in our practical deliberations about what to do, but this does not imply that the thing in question cannot be intrinsically valuable to any degree.

Of course, just because we can answer these three reasons for thinking that abstract objects could not be intrinsically valuable, it does not follow that they could be, let alone that they are. In order to draw that conclusion, we would need some kind of positive argument for it.

Here's an ambitious, speculative argument for this conclusion. First of all, we are considering the possibility that entities of these types might be intrinsically valuable *on the assumption that they exist*. After all, if something does not exist, then it cannot

---

30 Something like this argument is advanced by Anderson; see the discussion in Chapter 3, Section 1.
31 Something like this is suggested in Tännsjö 1999, p. 531.

be intrinsically valuable. But what does it mean to say that the number 7, for instance, exists? Well, it must mean, at a minimum, that there is a difference between a world containing the number 7 and an empty world that contains nothing. This difference between worlds would be reflected in the results of counting the number of entities in the world, or in the values of our bound variables.[32]

So let's consider two different worlds, a world containing the number 7 and a world containing nothing.[33] Which world seems better to you? It should come as no surprise, by now, how things seem to me: anything is better than nothing. But if the world containing the number 7 is better than the empty world, in what respect is it better? To what kind of value can we appeal in order to explain this apparent difference? Well, the only value that seems relevant is intrinsic value; no other kind of value has any possible application here. The world containing the number 7 includes an intrinsic structure that is lacking in the empty world, and this explains the difference in intrinsic value between them. I conclude that there is some reason, albeit a highly speculative and not at all demonstrative one, for thinking that abstract objects of type (4) have some degree of intrinsic value.[34]

To return to the main question of this chapter, namely, degrees of intrinsic value, we should ask whether numbers, sets, properties, and propositions differ from one another with respect to degrees of intrinsic value. When we consider one of these things relative to the other things of the same type, they all seem to be alike with respect to intrinsic value. The number 77, for instance, seems no more intrinsically valuable than the number 7. The set {1, 2, 3} seems no more intrinsically valuable than the set {2, 3, 4},

---

[32] Thus Quine's famous test of one's ontological commitment: "To be is to be the value of a variable" (Quine 1953, p. 15).
[33] These may not be possible worlds, of course, since the standard view is that the abstract objects in question exist necessarily if they exist at all (see, e.g., Plantinga 1974). But I don't see why this should prevent us from making the comparison in thought.
[34] This argument can be repeated for those other ontological categories that I am unable to discuss here because of limits of time and space.

and neither one of these sets seems more (or less!) intrinsically valuable than the null set. Possessing the property of being rational might make a concrete particular thing intrinsically valuable to a high degree, but the property itself, assuming that it exists apart from its instances, is no more intrinsically valuable than any other property, such as the property of being square. And the proposition *Snow is white* seems to be no more intrinsically valuable than the proposition that *Snow is black*.

I conclude that entities of type (4) have some degree of intrinsic value, however small, and that every entity in a given class has the same degree of intrinsic value as every other entity in that same class (assuming that these entities exist, of course). This concludes my discussion of entities of type (4).

Turning now to entities of type (3), abstract states of affairs, in Chapter 3 we saw that there was some reason to think that these things could be bearers of intrinsic value—if they existed, of course. Like everything else, they have intrinsic structures that distinguish them from one another, and these structures provide the basis for their intrinsic value.[35] But do different states of affairs possess different degrees of intrinsic value? To me, they also seem to be alike with respect to intrinsic value. For example, the state of affairs of someone's being happy seems no more intrinsically valuable than the state of affairs of someone's being miserable, as long as they are considered simply as abstract objects. This approach also has the virtue of answering, in one fell swoop, questions about the relative value of odd states of affairs such as disjunctive and negative states of affairs, questions that "tend to boggle the mind," as Törbjorn Tännsjö says.[36]

But some people object strongly to this idea. They hold that some abstract states of affairs are intrinsically better than others,

---

35 This account answers an objection from Adams (1999, p. 17), who suggests that states of affairs do not typically have the sort of unity required to be excellent. What we say about states of affairs here is similar to what we should say about the case of relations.

36 Tännsjö 1999, p. 533; this approach also has the virtue of treating states of affairs like propositions.

and perhaps also that some states of affairs are intrinsically bad.[37] Let's consider the following pair of abstract states of affairs, then: *an innocent person's being tortured*, on the one hand, and *a virtuous person's being rewarded*, on the other hand. Presumably many philosophers would say that the former is intrinsically bad, and the latter is intrinsically valuable. Could this be right?

If we consider these two things as existing, abstract states of affairs, it seems that these philosophers are quite mistaken. First of all, there is a big difference between these states of affairs existing and their obtaining; so far, I have said only that they exist, not that they obtain.[38] Assuming that they exist necessarily if they exist at all,[39] these same states of affairs exist in all possible worlds, even in worlds that contain no people at all. But in those worlds, why think that the one state of affairs is any better intrinsically than the other? Of course, it would be better for some actual virtuous person to be rewarded than for some actual innocent person to be tortured. But neither one of these things actually occurs in those possible worlds in which no people exist at all, so this is not a good reason to think that the abstract states of affairs themselves differ with respect to intrinsic value. These states are simply abstract structures, like propositions. But if they have the same degree of intrinsic value in worlds in which no people exist at all, how could they have a different intrinsic value in worlds in which they obtain? The intrinsic value of a thing depends only on those properties it possesses intrinsically.[40] I conclude that like entities of type (4), abstract states of affairs have some degree of intrinsic value, however small, and that they all possess it to the same degree.

---

37 See Chisholm 1986, p. 61, for example, or Lemos 1994, p. 15, and the discussion of Lemos in Chapter 3.
38 If they obtain, then they obtain in virtue of some arrangement of concrete things: see Lemos 1994, p. 21, and the comparison between truth for propositions and obtaining for states of affairs in Plantinga 1974, pp. 47–8.
39 As people typically do, and as one must if one thinks of possible worlds as maximal possible states of affairs (see Plantinga 1974, chapter 4, for instance).
40 For a similar argument, see the criticism of Lemos's view in Chapter 3, Section 1.

5. Concrete States and Pain

What about entities of type (2), concrete states of particular objects? In Chapter 3, we saw that there were reasons to think that they could be bearers of intrinsic value, and I have nothing to add to those positive arguments here. However, I should like to discuss here the claim that some concrete states of particular objects are intrinsically bad, such as the state of being in pain, since this claim has played such an important role in many discussions of intrinsic value.[41]

Pain is bad—that much seems clear; but in what way is pain bad? Clearly my pains are typically bad for me, either because they are unpleasant for me to experience, or because they might signal damage to my person, or because they interrupt my normal activities, projects, and plans. But just because my pains are bad for me, this is not sufficient, all by itself, to conclude that they are *intrinsically* bad.

Thomas Nagel argues that pain involves not just agent-relative, but also agent-neutral negative value.[42] He says that

> My objective attitude toward pain is rightly taken over from the immediate attitude of the subject, and naturally takes the form of an evaluation of the pain itself, rather than merely a judgment of what would be reasonable for its victim to want: "*This experience* ought not to go on, *whoever* is having it."[43]

Suppose that Nagel is right about the form of our attitudes toward pain.[44] Does it follow that the concrete state of being in pain is intrinsically bad?

---

41 This idea is central to the thought of Plato, Aristotle, Bentham, and Mill, just to name a few (see Zimmerman 2010). What I say about pain below could also be said, *mutatis mutandis*, about pleasure.
42 Actually, he finds this to be a self-evident truth (see Nagel 1986, pp. 159–60). For the sake of the argument, I shall consider Nagel's argument as an attempt to show that the concrete state of being in pain is intrinsically bad.
43 Nagel 1986, p. 161.
44 For a landmark essay in which this judgment is called into question on the basis of scientific studies of pain, see Dennett 1978; recent essays concerning the nature of pain can be found in Aydede 2006, and a helpful introduction to these issues is provided in Aydede 2010.

I'm not sure. We need to look carefully at what the state of being in pain involves. Pain occurs only as a state of some particular organism. Pain cannot exist in a vacuum, we might say; it must occur in some sentient subject, at some particular place and time.[45] And when considered as a state of some actual sentient subject, the state of being in pain clearly includes some components that are intrinsically good, including (perhaps) bare awareness, life, and the sentient subject itself. As St. Augustine said,

> The pain that beasts feel reveals a power that is amazing and praiseworthy in its own way, because it shows that even the souls of beasts have a strong drive toward unity in governing and animating their bodies. For what is pain but a sense of resistance to division and corruption?[46]

So although the state of being in pain certainly has some aspects that would provide fully informed, properly functioning valuers with reasons to avoid or prevent it, it also has other aspects that would provide fully informed, properly functioning valuers with reasons to value it for its own sake.

Some may feel that this argument involves a bit of cheating. They might wonder if we could isolate the really bad part of the state of being in pain in order to argue that this really bad part is intrinsically bad all by itself. So let's give this a try. Let's abstract the painfulness of some particular state of being in pain, subtracting the sentient subject and the particular details of the pain's causes and effects, separating in thought that which cannot be separated in fact.[47] Notice that when we do this, we leave behind at least some of the agent-relative badness of pain described above.

Once we do this, though, it is not clear that what we have isolated as a result of this process of abstraction actually exists. I have

---

45 In this respect, pain is like thought: just as there can be no free-floating thought without a thinker, there can be no pain without a subject to experience it.
46 St. Augustine 1993, p. 117.
47 Here we are following the lead of the Subtle Doctor: See Wolter's description of Scotus's doctrine of the Formal Distinction in Wolter 1967, pp. 431–2.

tried to remain steadfastly neutral about matters ontological so far, but it does strike me as a bit ontologically extravagant to posit in existence all three of the following things: (a) the sentient subject, (b) the state of the sentient subject's being in pain, and (c) the painfulness of the state of the sentient subject's being in pain. Unless someone has an argument for the conclusion that (c) exists, in addition to (a) and (b) (and I am aware of no such arguments), I think that we can safely set aside this line of inquiry.

But to return to the main question: even if the concrete state of being in pain includes some intrinsically valuable things as parts (such as the experiencing subject), it does not follow that the state as a whole is intrinsically good. With regard to the state of being in pain, perhaps the bad parts are more significant when compared to the good parts. So on balance, maybe there are good reasons to avoid or prevent pain, regardless of who its sentient subject happens to be, as Nagel pointed out. In other words, we may be faced with a case of organic disunity here, wherein the whole is worse that the sum of the values of the parts. Perhaps we should admit that the state of being in pain is intrinsically bad after all.

I'm not sure. But it seems important enough to register this uncertainty, given the virtually unanimous tradition according to which pain is intrinsically bad always and everywhere. I conclude that at least some concrete states of particular objects are intrinsically valuable to some degree. Like concrete particular objects themselves, these states are intrinsically valuable to different degrees, depending on their intrinsic structures.

6. Conclusion

Everything that exists has an intrinsic structure, a set of properties that it possesses intrinsically. Some intrinsic structures are intrinsically better than others, and this explains why things have the degrees of intrinsic value that they do.

Together with the arguments provided in Chapter 3, the arguments in the last two sections of this chapter complete my case for the Ambitious Speculative Conclusion, namely, the view that something in every exemplified ontological category is intrinsically valuable to some degree. If I am right about this conclusion, then a great many arguments about the bearers of intrinsic value are simply beside the point.

The arguments introduced in the first three sections of this chapter, together with the arguments provided in Chapters 2 and 4, advance my case for the Main Conclusion, the view that every concrete particular thing is intrinsically valuable to some degree. I will add to this case slightly in Chapter 6 before drawing it to a close in Chapter 7.

I must admit, though, that the account of degrees of intrinsic value developed in this chapter lacks one important, desirable ingredient: sharp criteria that would enable us to assign a specific degree of intrinsic value to every specific thing. I have already confessed that I have no such criteria to offer. Since the most strident objections to the application of the concept of intrinsic value without explicit criteria seem to come from people working in the area of ethics, I shall postpone a complete defense of a criterion-free approach to intrinsic value in the face of such objections to the next chapter, where I shall take up the relationship between intrinsic value and ethics.

6 Ethics

In the Introduction, I mentioned a familiar distinction between conclusive reasons for doing things (which specify one's obligations "all things considered"), and overridable reasons for doing things (which specify an initial presumption in favor of doing something). In this chapter, I argue that the Main Conclusion implies that we have overridable reasons for treating all things with some degree of respect, since respect is the appropriate response to that which ought to be valued for its own sake.[1]

A number of authors have presented arguments designed to show that the concept of intrinsic value is not ethically significant. In Section 1 of this chapter, I consider arguments to the effect that unless we have explicit criteria that enable us to distinguish what is intrinsically valuable from everything else, facts about intrinsic value are useless for ethical purposes. Section 2 will be devoted to arguments based on the alleged logical gap in between *X is intrinsically valuable* and *X is to be preserved, respected, etcetera*. In Section 3, I shall consider the objection that if facts about intrinsic value were ethically relevant, then they would make our ethical obligations too numerous or otherwise unbearable. Finally, in Section 4, I shall make some concluding observations about ethical goodness and the idea of treating everything with respect.

1. Do We Need Explicit Criteria?
A number of authors have argued that without explicit criteria for the application of the concept of intrinsic value, it has "no useful employment,"[2] and that the advice to take intrinsic value into

---

[1] Although historically the concept of intrinsic value has often been linked with utilitarianism (in the work of Mill and Moore, for instance), in this chapter I shall show that it need not be in order to be ethically serious.

[2] Westacott 1994, p. 177.

consideration is "empty."[3] Elliot Sober, for instance, wonders what the difference is between a mountain and a highway in virtue of which someone might argue that the mountain deserves to be protected, unlike the highway.[4] These two things do not differ with respect to having wants, interests, or preferences, for instance. The difference is not in their history, because each one is constructed (in some form or fashion); nor is the difference that one is natural and the other is artificial. Finally, it does not help us to appeal here to what things need:

> Suppose one says that an object needs something if the object will cease to exist if it does not get it. Then species, plants, and mountain ranges do have needs, but only in the sense that automobiles, garbage dumps, and buildings do too. If everything has needs, the advice to take needs into account in ethical deliberation is empty, unless it is supplemented by some technique for weighting and comparing the needs of different objects.[5]

Calling this "The Demarcation Problem," he argues further that

> An environmentalist theory shares with all ethical theories an interest in not saying that everything has autonomous value. The reason this position is proscribed is that it makes the adjudication of ethical conflict very difficult indeed. (In addition, it is radically implausible, but we can set that objection to one side.[6])

Nicholas Agar seems to agree. Echoing the worries of Jana Thompson,[7] Agar defends the importance of answering the Cutoff Question, saying that

> We need to draw and defend the moral significance of a boundary between living and nonliving things to prevent

---

3 Sober 1986, p. 239. Hereafter, page citations refer to Sober 1986.
4 Sober, pp. 243ff., commenting on Routley and Routley 1979.
5 Sober, p. 239.
6 Sober, p. 239.
7 See Thompson 1990.

our life ethic from degenerating into an everything ethic. If absolutely everything is to be special, then gone will be any moral incentive to look out for nature. What grounds then would permit us to limit inherent worth, or intrinsic value, to biological objects, thereby marking off the microbe's good from the nonbiological carbonate formation's and ice crystal's good?[8]

To summarize, then, if we have no criteria that we can use to identify that which has intrinsic value, then the ethical advice to take intrinsic value into consideration in our ethical deliberation will be empty, and we will be unable to adjudicate ethical conflicts.

In Chapter 5, I identified a number of judgments concerning comparative intrinsic value, including judgments about large classes of things, judgments that seem warranted in the absence of sharp criteria that would enable us to assign a precise degree of intrinsic value to every intrinsic structure. I also provided an explanation of these cases in terms of the inclusion of one kind of structure within another one. These kinds of judgments would certainly help us to adjudicate some conflicts of interest. This is because, typically, when we are trying to decide what to do, we need to know not the exact degree of intrinsic value possessed by some particular thing X or how X compares to every other thing in existence, but rather how X compares to some other particular thing, Y. St. Augustine was surely right, for instance, to chide a child for preferring the continued existence of a pet parrot to the destruction of a human being.[9] It is also worth noting that some of these authors seem to presuppose that intrinsic value cannot come in degrees; as we have seen, though, this common assumption is simply unwarranted.[10]

Finally, some of these authors are criticizing the attempt to use the concept of intrinsic value all by itself to construct something like a complete environmental ethic, one goal of which would be to enable us to make practical decisions about what to do in all

---

8   Agar 2001, p. 68.
9   See St. Augustine 1993, p. 82.
10 See Chapter 2, Section 2.

possible cases of conflict.[11] But I am not trying to provide anything like this—my goal is much less ambitious; I am just trying to show that my Main Conclusion is ethically serious, and that it can make a difference in our ordinary ethical deliberations.

It is not the case that if we cannot provide sharp criteria that would enable us to assign a precise degree of intrinsic value to every intrinsic structure, then considerations of intrinsic value are completely useless for ethics. Noting that we often wrongly dismiss nonsentient things from our ethical deliberations "simply because they cannot be counted or given weight in our calculations in any obvious way," Stephen Clark suggests that we "reject this kind of systematic approach to the problem," and that ethical systems that attempt to provide precise calculations of what should be done "present a sort of ghastly reduction *ad absurdum* of their own pretensions."[12] Clark is right; the demand that one's ethical theory be "computationally tractable" in the sense of providing "a feasible algorithm, or a series of steps, intelligible by humans, leading to the action prescribed by the theory" (without ever giving us the wrong answer) sets the bar too high.[13]

This response to the problem of criteria also suggests a response to Fred Feldman, who argues that if we characterize the intrinsically valuable as that which is good simply in virtue of its intrinsic nature (as I have done, roughly), then there will be more than one species of intrinsic value, including moral, logical, epistemic, and aesthetic value.[14] I have some reservations about the details of this argument,[15] but suppose that it is correct. Feldman then draws

---

11 There may be good reasons to doubt that any plausible ethical theory can generate a reliable decision procedure like this; see Nagel 1986, p. 162, for instance.
12 Clark 1977, pp. 54, 187.
13 This is Daniel Dennett's catchy formulation of the demand, which he himself endorses: see Dennett 1996, p. 154.
14 Feldman 1998, p. 351.
15 For instance, given my assignment of a degree of intrinsic value to abstract objects (see Chapter 5, Section 3), it might turn out that moral, logical, and epistemic kinds of intrinsic value are actually reducible to the intrinsic value of abstract objects (if they exist). Aesthetic value, by contrast, does not strike me as a kind of intrinsic value. Since arguing this point would take me too far afield, I shall not develop it here.

the conclusion that intrinsic value must not be the central unifying principle of ethics, by means of which everything else can be defined, contrary to Moore. Moore would then "have to say more: what is distinctive about the distinctively ethical sort of intrinsic goodness?"[16] Even if Feldman were right about this, I should not find it troubling, since I'm not trying to develop a complete ethical theory here, let alone trying to do so in terms of the notion of intrinsic value all by itself.[17]

In the final Section of this chapter, I shall discuss some of the ways in which one might respect the intrinsic value of everything even though one did not possess explicit criteria for degrees of intrinsic value or a reliable formula for computing which actions to perform. I shall not unveil a complete ethical theory at that point, of course, but I shall argue that the intrinsic values of things should make a difference to us ethically even without such a theory. First, though, it is important to consider the alleged logical gap in between *X is intrinsically valuable* and *X ought to be preserved, respected, etcetera*.

2. A Logical Gap?

Mark Bernstein complains that my kind of approach to intrinsic value (like the approaches of Moore, Ross, Brentano and Chisholm) "leaves the nature of the intrinsically valuable mysterious."[18] Because of this, he claims that we need an argument to show that the possession of the intrinsically valuable "makes one better off or more morally worthy" than otherwise and an argument "to demonstrate why items with intrinsic value deserve to be chosen or promoted."[19] Otherwise, for all we know, what is intrinsically

---

16 Feldman 1998, p. 351.
17 I do not claim that all values are reducible to intrinsic value, or that the so-called Regress Argument for the existence of intrinsic value is sound. This argument is discussed in Rescher 1982, an Aristotelian version is defended in Routley and Routley 1979, and such arguments are criticized in Conee 1982.
18 Bernstein 2001, p. 337. See also the discussion of Bernstein in Chapter 2, Section 6.
19 Bernstein 2001, p. 339. In a similar vein, John Laird notes that "intrinsic values might well occur without being amenable to search, and are therefore not ends" (Laird 1929, pp. 43–9, quoted in Carter 1979, p. 39).

valuable might not be good for us to possess, or might even be bad for us; such a value, according to Bernstein, would not be a kind of value "worth the name."[20]

Since we should not take an anthropocentric approach to intrinsic value,[21] we should bite Bernstein's bullet: there could be intrinsically valuable things that were not good for us to possess (or even bad for us). In Chapter 5, Section 3, I discussed John O'Neill's cases involving dictatorships and viruses, and concluded that these were not persuasive examples of intrinsically bad things. But perhaps a more difficult kind of case, suggested by Bernstein's arguments, would involve machines that are designed only to produce bad effects on human beings, like land mines or machines of torture or nuclear weapons. If what I said about degrees of intrinsic value in the previous Chapter is true, then doesn't it follow that a nuclear weapon might be just as intrinsically valuable as a computer-operated artificial heart, for example?

Yes, it does follow. And so we have an overridable reason to preserve both machines in existence. But in the case of the nuclear weapon, in addition to its intrinsic value, there are other reasons involving its instrumental value (or disvalue) that bear on the decision to preserve it in existence, such as its potential for destruction. Hence the overridable reason for preserving the nuclear weapon is actually overridden; it should be destroyed (or disarmed, at least).[22] Of course, the overridable reason for preserving the artificial heart might be overridden too, although different kinds of considerations will be relevant to that decision. In both cases, though, we are dealing with objects that have some degree of intrinsic value, and this provides us with an overridable reason for preserving them. So Bernstein's complaint about my kind of approach to intrinsic value seems to reduce to the claim that it implies that not every intrinsically valuable thing need be instrumentally valuable for human beings, but there is nothing objectionable about this consequence.

---

20 Bernstein 2001, p. 340.
21 See Chapter 5, Section 2.
22 Thanks to Ben Bradley for helping me to express this point clearly.

In a related vein, Tom Regan appeals to Ockham's Razor, arguing that positing some degree of intrinsic value in all things is "superfluous at best" when it comes to "illuminating, accounting for or grounding our duties to nature."[23] There is no logical connection, he claims, between *X is intrinsically valuable* and *X should be respected*.[24] By contrast, Robert Audi claims that it would be "inexplicable" to admit that something is intrinsically valuable, and then to deny that there is a reason to seek or promote it.[25] What's a person to make of these diametrically opposed claims?

Something is intrinsically valuable if and only if it is good in itself, if and only if it possesses an intrinsic structure which would lead fully informed, properly functioning valuers to value it for its own sake. Those who believe that human beings are intrinsically valuable think that such value provides us with a reason to respect them. It would be sheer speciesism to deny that the intrinsic value of other things fails to provide a reason to respect them, once we admit that this reason is only as strong as the degree of intrinsic value present.[26] So given the way that I am using the phrase *intrinsic value* in this book, I share Audi's sense that it would be "inexplicable" to admit that something is intrinsically valuable, but then to deny that there was a reason to seek or promote it.[27]

If every concrete particular thing has an intrinsic structure that provides us with some reason to value it for its own sake, then doesn't this mean that we are literally overwhelmed with ends to consider in our actions? And if we are, does this mean that we really

---

23 This is because a hierarchy of means would generate the same duties without positing intrinsic values (Regan 1992, p. 178); of course, even if this is so, I take myself to have provided independent reasons for thinking that nature has intrinsic value.
24 Regan 1992, p. 179.
25 Audi 1997, pp. 135–54; for a similar claim, see Adams 1999, p. 25. Bernstein discusses Audi's claim in Bernstein 2001, p. 343, fn. 11.
26 Thanks to Mark Murphy for suggesting this argument to me (in correspondence), modeled on the argument concerning the Cutoff Question developed in Chapter 4.
27 As Adams says, "assertions of value and obligation do express attitudes involving motivation" (Adams 1999, p. 25); see also Dancy's discussion of Ross in Dancy 2005, p. 37. Intrinsic value, then, turns out to be what Bernstein elsewhere calls a "morally relevant property" (see Bernstein 2002, p. 531ff.).

have no obligation to consider intrinsic values in our ethical deliberations at all? These questions are the topics of the next section.

3. Impossible Demands?

Owen Flanagan defends something he calls the Principle of Minimal Psychological Realism: "Make sure that when constructing a moral theory or projecting a moral ideal that the character, decision processing, and behavior prescribed are possible, or are perceived to be possible, for creatures like us."[28] Simple formulations of act utilitarianism fail the test, for example, because they are too demanding, requiring "an impossible amount of attention to one's action options."[29]

Roderick Nash considers the ever-broadening scope of ethical theories over the sweep of human history, and extrapolates inductively to the conclusion that future ethical theories will come to include everything in their scope, include inanimate objects.[30] According to Agar, such a development would generate a "profusion of end conflicts": every arrangement of matter would be valuable, but so would the result of any change; hence we would have no particular obligations at all.[31]

Taken together, Flanagan's principle and Agar's observation seem to suggest that the intrinsic value of everything would eliminate, rather than introduce, ethical obligations to inanimate objects. But this appearance is misleading. We are literally surrounded by intrinsically valuable things, but some things are clearly more intrinsically valuable than others. To return to one of my earlier examples, it seems clear that a human being is more intrinsically valuable than a slug. And in cases in which we are able to consider intrinsic values alone because other things appear to be equal, these kinds of judgments are relevant, and they do provide us with some guidance.

For instance, suppose that I have a broken sewing machine. It may make very little difference, in terms of consequences for

---

28 Flanagan 1991, p. 32; quoted in Agar 2001, p. 154.
29 Flanagan 1991, pp. 33–4.
30 See Nash 1989.
31 Agar 2001, p. 168.

living things, whether I get it fixed or throw it away and buy a new one. Some environmentalists will insist (appealing again to some version of consequentialism) that there is a lot of pollution caused by the manufacture and shipping of new machines, and of course this fact does deserve to be considered. But buying a new machine also involves benefits to those people associated with the manufacturing company, and this must be considered too. For the sake of the argument, let's simply stipulate that in this particular case, the consequences of the two alternative actions for living things are roughly comparable, as far as we can tell. But the intrinsic value of the machine itself provides me with an overridable reason to respect it, and one way of showing respect would be to get it fixed. In the absence of any good reasons to the contrary, this overridable reason should make a difference in my ethical deliberations.[32]

Or suppose that as you walk down the sidewalk, you notice a line of ants in your path. Imagine that there is no reason to think that these ants are causing any harm to any person, animal, or structure, so that you have no reason to think that their presence is instrumentally bad. Should you take extra care not to step on any of them, or should you simply continue in your present path, probably stepping on several ants in the process? The intrinsic value of the ants provides you with a good reason to avoid stepping on them out of respect.[33]

Agar says that "We may be happy intoning the phrase *All life is precious*, but we certainly feel in no way committed to heroic blade-of-grass rescue acts."[34] This is true, of course, but it does not show that blades of grass are not intrinsically valuable. It shows only that we have limited time and resources, and that we recognize

---

[32] Of course, getting the machine fixed might require the destruction of other things of intrinsic value, introducing more complexity to the decision. As indicated above, I am not trying to offer a formula here that would enable us to determine the right action in any particular situation.

[33] The exemplary life of St. Francis of Assisi comes to mind here; see White 1967, where it is suggested that St. Francis be considered the patron saint of the environment.

[34] Agar 2001, p. 64.

that blades of grass do not possess a very high degree of intrinsic value. But if we had unlimited time and unlimited resources, what then? Perhaps we might actually make efforts to preserve individual blades of grass. In that case, our rescues of blades of grass might not count as *heroic*, since the concept of a heroic rescue seems to presuppose some kind of sacrifice, but that doesn't seem to be essential to Agar's argument.

If we were to adopt some version of consequentialism according to which we are always obligated to maximize the intrinsic value in the world, then I believe that Flanagan and Agar's objections would give us pause, but I am not even tempted in this direction. I have claimed only that the intrinsic value of something provides us with an overridable reason for treating it with respect, and I am not trying to develop a complete ethical theory here, let alone a system that would enable us to resolve all conflicts. Instead, in the next Section, I shall offer some comparatively simple advice.

4. On Symbolic Goodness and Respect

Robert Adams notes that historically, ethical theories have tended to stress only one of two very different things: loving the good, on the one hand, and doing one's duty, on the other hand.[35] Like Adams (and Plato), I wish to emphasize here the importance of loving the good, especially the intrinsically valuable. We should aim to treat everything and everyone with appropriate respect, given what they are, all other things being equal.

Typically, treating something with respect involves promoting and preserving it. But this is not always so; respect for a gravely ill person might lead one to wish that he die quickly and mercifully, for instance.[36] As Thomas Scanlon says, "understanding the value

---

[35] Adams 1999, p. 14. Although some details differ, my arguments in this Section are heavily indebted to the discussion in Adams 1999, to which page citations refer hereafter.

[36] This example is due to Anderson: see Anderson 1993, p. 26; see also Anderson 1993, pp. 8–16, Rabinowicz and Rønnow-Rasmussen 1999, pp. 45–8, and Scanlon 1998, pp. 79–100.

of something often involves not merely knowing that it is valuable or how valuable it is, but also how it is to be valued."[37]

Before saying more about trying to treat everything with respect, I need to discuss the nature of ethical demands in general. One thing that distinguishes the properly functioning human being from (nearly?) everything else in the world is the ability to distinguish what is good from what is bad, and to be for the good and against the bad.[38] Now one way to be for the good is to contribute causally to its existence intentionally. If one contributes causally to the existence of some good thing actively but not intentionally, then this is not an example of the distinctively human capacity I have in mind; after all, we promote the existence of many things in this way without even realizing it. Intentions are necessary as well. But contributing causally to the existence of the good intentionally is not the only way to be for the good; it is also possible to be for the good symbolically. Let me explain.

Being for some good symbolically requires that one have the intention to contribute causally to its existence where feasible,[39] but it does not require success in carrying out this intention. Being for some good X symbolically also requires the disposition to formulate thoughts (and associated attitudes) of the form "X is good," "X should be respected," "X should be promoted," and so on. Finally, it involves also a disposition to communicate these thoughts (and associated attitudes) to others in the appropriate circumstances. So being for the good symbolically involves two things: an objective element, one's recognition of some particular good, and a conventional one, the meanings of one's actions and utterances.[40] Although

---

37 Scanlon 1998, p. 100.
38 See the discussion of symbolic action and convention in Adams, Chapter 9. Unlike Adams, though, I am not optimistic about locating any single actual thing that would best fit the role of "The Good" in a Platonic sense; see Adams, pp. 20ff.
39 Where being feasible requires that success in such causal contribution is reasonable to expect, not just possible. Adams makes a similar point about expectations in Adams, p. 220, and about the necessity of the disposition to act in the concrete, p. 228.
40 Assuming, of course, that one is able so to communicate. See the brief discussion of the value of martyrdom and truth in Adams, p. 217, and the connection between morality and expression on p. 218.

recent ethical theories[41] have tended to emphasize doing one's duty through contributing causally to the existence of the good intentionally, being an ethically good person primarily involves being for the good symbolically, whether or not one is able to make such a difference in the world.[42]

In fact, sometimes these two things, one's being for the good symbolically and one's attempts to contribute causally to the existence of the good, pull in opposite directions. On June 11, 1963, Thich Quang Duc burned himself to death at a busy intersection in Saigon in order to draw attention to the repressive practices of the Catholic Diem regime in South Vietnam.[43] In order to identify symbolically with the good of his fellow monks (among others), he felt compelled to burn himself to death, thereby causing the death of a monk (namely, himself). Duc apparently felt that being symbolically for the good in this way was more important than contributing causally to his own flourishing.

Now some have argued, appealing implicitly to some kind of consequentialism, that this dramatic act was good because it made important causal contributions to the promotion of the good in question, thanks largely to the widespread distribution of a famous photograph of the event. But this strikes me as largely irrelevant to judging the value of Duc's action. Even if it had led to no positive changes in the world, still his costly display of symbolic devotion to the good would count significantly toward a positive ethical assessment of him as a person.

Returning now to the topic of the intrinsic value of everything, it would be impossible indeed to be ethically good if this required

---

41 Recent in the sense of modern, that is; utilitarianism and other varieties of consequentialism are paradigm cases of what I am talking about here, whereas the recent interest in virtue theories represents a welcome retreat from it (see Adams, p. 219).

42 As Adams says (Adams, p. 217, for example); see also his discussion of helplessness on pp. 224, 227. Otherwise, there would be too much moral luck (see Davison 1999a and 1999b, Feinberg 1962, and Nagel 1976). In Chapter 7, I shall describe an interesting connection between moral goodness, gratitude, and worship, which is a way of being symbolically for the good (among other things).

43 See Topmiller 1999.

promoting and preserving in existence every intrinsically valuable thing. After all, it is impossible to preserve everything in existence; the simple acts of breathing, eating, and moving one's body result in the destruction of many living and nonliving things, whereas the cessation of these activities would result in one's own death.[44] But if I am right about the importance of symbolic value, then part of what it means to be ethically good is that one show respect for everything at least symbolically, whether or not one succeeds in promoting and preserving all things in existence.

Typically, we must decide how to act in a given situation based upon many different factors, and there is no completely reliable formula to which we can appeal. We must consider the consequences of our actions, insofar as we can determine what they would be, in terms of both the intrinsic and instrumental values that seem to be at stake. But we should also consider how our actions symbolically respect or fail to respect the intrinsic value at stake in the situation.

For example, Kazuko Okakura reports that:

> Our legends ascribe the first flower arrangement to those early Buddhist saints who gathered the flowers strewn by a storm and, in their infinite solicitude for all living things, placed them in vessels of water.[45]

The symbolic respect for the flowers evinced by these saints was highly appropriate even though their actions made very little difference to the fate of the flowers.

Here is another example. Suppose that you have a pet dog, and it becomes clear that the dog suffers from a painful terminal illness that cannot be cured. You are faced with a difficult decision. In terms of the consequences involved in this situation, you will probably conclude at some point that your dog's life should be

---

44 See Adams 1999, p. 26. It is interesting to note here the discrepancy between the two accounts of the creation of human beings in the book of Genesis in the Hebrew scriptures, only one of which sanctions the consumption of animal flesh as food; see Linzey 1995.

45 Okakura 1962, pp. 92–4, 101.

terminated. But there are many different ways to do this, some of which would involve more symbolic respect for the intrinsic value of the dog than others,[46] and there would be something ethically defective about you if you did not pay attention to these differences in your deliberations.

More generally, where it is feasible, we should try to show respect for the apparent intrinsic value of everything we are able to consider. Having come of age in our anthropocentric culture, we may find it difficult even to consider such things. I myself do not claim to be a person who has fully integrated respect for the intrinsic value of everything into my life. Probably things would have been easier for me in this regard if I had been immersed from childhood in a culture in which one thought that

> To savor the majestic roar of a waterfall, the subtle sounds of pebbles washing over pebbles in a man-made pot-hole next to a Japanese Inn, or the irregularity of a garden rock, or the perfect symmetry of a single flower, or the colour, texture and smell of tree bark in spring is to gain immediate positive value experiences which are never repeated, and yet are generally predictable as sources of profound value.[47]

Even though I am not a completely integrated person in this respect, given the importance of being symbolically for the good and the fact that this involves the willingness to communicate one's thoughts and attitudes to others, there is a sense in which hypocrisy may be the lesser of two evils here. By hypocrisy, I mean simply a lack of fit between the ethical ideals that one endorses publicly, on the one hand, and the ethical progress that one is able to achieve in one's private life. (This definition is intended to

---

[46] Your decision will no doubt also reflect the instrumental value of the dog to you, since by hypothesis the dog is your pet, but my point is that this should not be the only consideration.

[47] Carter 1979, p. 49. According to my view, then, being immersed in such a culture would constitute a case of positive moral luck: see the references in footnote 43, and Berry's comments on the love of the particular and the problems introduced by classification in science in Berry 2001.

distinguish hypocrisy from deception pure and simple, wherein one has no intention of doing in one's private ethical life what one advocates publicly.[48]) Let me explain.

Suppose that I am convinced that everything is intrinsically valuable to some degree, but I find myself unable to show respect for things in many situations, thanks to years of acting habitually as if nearly everything around me were intrinsically neutral. Would it be better for me to keep my views about intrinsic value to myself in this situation, or to make them known to others, knowing all the while that I am unable (presently, at least) to live in a manner that evinces the proper respect for all things? If I keep my views to myself, then there are at least two important respects in which I will be deficient in being symbolically for the good, namely, (1) by not having a firm intention to contribute causally to its existence where feasible, and (2) by suppressing the disposition to communicate my thoughts (and associated attitudes) concerning the good to others. By contrast, if I communicate my views about the good to others, then I will be deficient in only one of these respects. In this sense, hypocrisy seems to be the lesser of two evils.

5. Conclusion

This completes my brief discussion of the ethical implications of my Main Conclusion, the view that everything is intrinsically valuable to some degree. As I have said repeatedly, I have not tried to offer a complete ethical theory here, or a rule that would enable a person to determine the right action to perform in any specific situation. Instead, I have suggested that the intrinsic values of things should play some role in our ethical deliberations, and that the significance of those considerations will vary from situation to situation. This is enough to establish the ethical seriousness of the Main Conclusion.

Despite everything I have said in this chapter, I expect that some readers will feel that when all is said and done, the intrinsic value of everything actually makes no practical difference at all

---

48 For a different conception of hypocrisy and a discussion of related ideas, see Spiegel 1999.

in the deliberations of the ethically good person, so that my rather minimal ethical advice is actually empty. In response to this worry, I have a practical reply rather than a theoretical one. In this matter, as in so many things in life, the proof seems to be in the pudding, so to speak. Try to consider the intrinsic value of everything in your life and see what it is like. I predict that you will notice a difference over time in your relationship to the world around you, and that you will begin to notice and appreciate intrinsic value in unexpected places as a result of this attempt.

7 Theism and Intrinsic Value

The major theistic religions (Judaism, Christianity, and Islam) are devoted to the worship of an all-powerful, all-knowing, perfectly good God. I am not advocating that people who do not already believe in the existence of God become theists,[1] but the following question seems philosophically interesting whether or not one believes in God: What difference, if any, would it make for the Main Conclusion that I have defended in this book if theism were true? I shall divide this question into two parts, considering whether God's existence makes a difference for the ontology of intrinsic value in the first two sections, and then exploring ethical matters in the final section.

1. A Theistic Ontology of Intrinsic Value?

Many theists have thought that there is an intimate connection between God and goodness; some have even suggested that God is the Good.[2] To paraphrase the dilemma made famous by Plato's dialogue *Euthyphro*, are things intrinsically valuable just because God values them for their own sakes, or does God value things for their own sakes because they are already intrinsically valuable on their own?[3]

Of course, it is one thing to claim that God's creative activity is responsible for the existence of created things, as all traditional

---

1 In general, I think that religious belief is something over which we exercise little voluntary control, but discussing this question would take me far afield, so I shall set it aside here.
2 See the helpful discussion in MacDonald 1991b.
3 Walhout apparently tries to have it both ways (Walhout 1978, pp. 181–2), without much success.

theists hold,[4] but quite another thing to claim that God's valuing activity is responsible for their goodness. Should theists hold that God's valuing activity is responsible for the world's intrinsic value?

Theists who claim that God's valuing activity *is* responsible for the world's intrinsic value will hold that a given concrete particular thing is intrinsically valuable to some degree if and only if God values it for its own sake to that same degree. But theists who claim that God's valuing activity *is not* responsible for the world's intrinsic value will say the same thing, since they will believe that God is a fully informed, properly functioning valuer (and necessarily so). Both parties in this dispute will view God as an ideal valuer in the literal sense, since necessarily, God is as fully informed as possible and God functions as properly as possible. In fact, for theists, it would make sense to say that God would know the precise degree of intrinsic value possessed by everything. For the sake of convenience, let's say that theists who claim that God's valuing activity is responsible for the world's intrinsic value are embracing Divine Subjectivism about Intrinsic Value (DSIV). For reasons that will become clear, DSIV represents a challenging alternative to the picture I have developed in this book, so I should like to consider it in some detail.

John Brentlinger claims that "according to Christian thought, in the act of creation, God gives the standards by which the world and everything in it are to be judged." Furthermore,

> The love of the Christian God, according to [Anders] Nygren (and in Paul's epistles and the parables of Jesus) is not measured out in terms of some antecedently given scale of values. The values of things, in relation to God, are dependent, in

---

[4] Traditionally, creation includes three elements: bringing the world into existence from nothing initially, continually sustaining it in being from moment to moment, and cooperating with the exercise of the causal powers of all secondary causes; for more on this, see the helpful collection of essays in Morris 1988. I shall not discuss here God's creative relationship to abstract entities (but for a discussion of some of the difficulties involved in viewing God's creative activity as causally responsible for the existence of abstract entities, see Davison 1991).

this sense: the love of God creates the intrinsic value which belongs to the objects of his creation. It is not something which merely pertains to good things, that they should be loved by God. Being good and being God-loved, are essentially the same.[5]

This exposition of Christian thought certainly suggests some version of DSIV.[6]

In addition, the development of traditional theism in the Christian West during the medieval period was deeply influenced by a very short treatise composed by the early Christian and Neo-Platonic philosopher, Boethius. In it, he asks whether concrete particular substances would be good if they existed in a world without the Prime Good, God. Noting that it is possible to separate by a mental process two things which cannot be separated in actual fact, he asks us to consider the things that we regard as actually good in our world, and to imagine what they would be like if (*per impossibile*) they existed apart from God. His conclusion seems to be that such things would not be good at all, since goodness is had by participation, and only God is simple.[7]

Probably Boethius does not use the expression *good* to signify the same thing that I signify by using the expression *intrinsic value*, so perhaps it is unfair to him to consider his argument here as an argument for DSIV. But it does seem to me that he draws the wrong conclusion, if we consider his argument as applied to intrinsic value. For example, consider some particular human

---

5 Brentlinger 1970, p. 144.
6 I have some doubts about Nygren's analysis. To express just one of them, Jesus is reported as telling the twelve disciples not to be afraid for the following reason: "Are not two sparrows sold for a small coin? Yet not one of them falls to the ground without your Father's knowledge. Even all the hairs of your head are counted. So do not be afraid; you are worth more than many sparrows" (Matthew 10:29–31, NAB). To me, this seems incompatible with Divine Subjectivism about Intrinsic Value.
7 Boethius 1983, pp. 129–30. I think that this is his conclusion; I am not a Boethius scholar. For discussions of the intricate and sophisticated medieval debate generated by Boethius's short treatise, see the excellent collection of essays in MacDonald 1991A.

being, such as my ten year old son Benjamin, and imagine him existing apart from God (*per impossibile*?[8]). It seems to me that he would have just as much intrinsic value in such a situation as he would in a world in which God existed. A fully informed, properly functioning valuer focusing only on his intrinsic structure would value him to the same degree in both situations. If this were not so, then his intrinsic value would depend on something extrinsic to him, so that the ideal valuer would not be tracking *intrinsic* value in Boethius's thought experiment.

This same objection would apply with equal force against a Platonic account of intrinsic value in terms of participation. But what about an account of intrinsic value that does not understand goodness in terms of participation, yet still recognizes God as the transcendent Good? Here I shall consider briefly the account along these lines offered by Robert Adams, according to which excellence consists in a kind of resemblance to God.[9]

According to Adams, following Plato, we can be competent users of the word *good* without knowing the nature of goodness; after all, *water* refers to H_2O, but does not mean H_2O.[10] God is the transcendent Good, that which best plays the role of the referent of *the Good*.[11]

God is a particular, not a Platonic Form or universal; but God is the Good, and so Adams suggests that the excellence of created things might consist in some kind of resemblance of God.[12] This account has several advantages, he says; I shall not mention all of them here. One important advantage is that resemblance is grounded in the thing itself by "having parts of its grounds in each of the resembling things," and another is that resemblance is

---

8 Some (but not all) theists will regard this as metaphysically impossible, because they conceive of God as a metaphysically necessary being (see Plantinga 1974, for example).
9 Adams 1999; see also Kretzmann 1991B. Adams's larger notion of excellence seems to include the notion of the intrinsically valuable (see Adams 1999, pp. 14ff, especially pp. 19, 29), but Kretzmann's may not.
10 Adams 1999, pp. 15–16.
11 Adams 1999, p. 23.
12 Adams 1999, pp. 28ff.

objective, the sort of thing that an objective observer could notice (and this is part of the role picked out by *good*).[13]

Adams explicitly rejects DSIV as an answer to the Euthyphro-style question raised above:

> Supposing that excellent finite things are indeed loved by God, we may well think nonetheless that their excellence must consist, not in God's attitude toward them, but in something in them that grounds God's attitude, or provides God with a reason for it. For excellence should have grounds in the nature or condition of the excellent thing.[14]

How would Adams respond to the argument mentioned above by way of criticism of Boethius's thought experiment?[15] I argued that if my son Benjamin existed in a world apart from God, he would still be as intrinsically valuable as he would in a world containing God. Adams notes that if we assume that his account of excellence is correct (in the sense that God actually exists and God is the best candidate for playing the role of the Good), then there are two things that we might say about a world in which nothing like God existed:

> (A1) In such a world, nothing would resemble God and nothing would be excellent, although things in that world might have some other property instead, perhaps even a property "qualitatively indistinguishable from our concept of excellence."[16]

> (A2) Excellence in all possible worlds is determined by conformity to the standard in the actual world, namely, God – and God's existence is metaphysically necessary.[17]

---

13 Adams 1999, p. 29.
14 Adams 1999, p. 35.
15 Many thanks to Michael Bergmann for helpful correspondence concerning the relationship between Adams's notion of excellence and my notion of intrinsic value.
16 Adams 1999, pp. 46; this is what Hilary Putnam would say about people on Twin Earth, who interact with a substance XYZ that they call 'water' (see Putnam 1975).
17 Adams 1999, pp. 46–7.

Adams prefers the second response, (A2), even though it simply denies that the envisaged scenario is metaphysically possible. But this does not prevent us from considering it, and Adams declines to offer any reasons for thinking that God is necessary in this sense.

Adams finds the first reply, (A1), less appealing than the second because he is inclined to think that "it should not be a contingent matter what it would be excellent to be like."[18] I agree completely with this assessment, of course, since Adams conceives of excellence in such a way that it is very close to my conception of intrinsic value. In his final comments designed to introduce the relationship between excellence and the Good, he suggests that excellence for created things consists in the intersection of two different kinds of qualities:

> There are features by virtue of which things resemble God, and features that could serve as reasons for God's love. It is features that have both qualifications that will constitute excellence.[19]

Later, he says that "If there is a sacredness of finite persons, it is a derivative or secondary sacredness that belongs to them as images of the transcendent Good."[20] But now the problem stares us plainly in the face: Adams's account implies that if (*per impossibile*) Benjamin existed in a world without God, then he would not resemble God and hence would not have excellence. But then Benjamin's excellence does not depend exclusively on Benjamin himself – it depends also on whether or not God exists – contrary to Adams's description of excellence. I conclude that Adams's account of excellence in terms of resemblance to God is not a viable alternative to the account developed earlier in this book.

Of course, if theism is true, then God's creative activity is responsible for the existence of created things, as noted above, and hence for the fact that they possess the properties they do intrinsically.

---

18 Adams 1999, pp. 46–7.
19 Adams 1999, p. 36.
20 Adams 1999, p. 107. On p. 116, he speaks of the value and special sacredness of persons in the same breath.

So God's creative activity is causally responsible for the actual distribution of intrinsic value in the world. But God's valuing activity cannot be responsible for the fact that a given thing is intrinsically valuable; only the properties that it possesses intrinsically can be relevant to this. Those who would suggest otherwise owe us an alternative explanation of the sense of *intrinsic value*.[21]

Leibniz would agree with my rejection of DSIV, since he argues that the goodness of created things in general does not depend upon God's valuing them. He offers two arguments for this conclusion.[22] First, he claims that if God's valuing were to make created things good, then our praise for creation would become empty, since we could have offered the very same praise for God's having done something completely different instead. Had God decided that an awful world full of intense suffering and ugliness would be intrinsically valuable to a high degree, for instance, then the same praise that theists offer to God for the goodness of the actual world could still be appropriately offered for this imaginary, awful world. But this seems mistaken: in order for praise to be meaningful, it must be discriminating in the sense that it is tracks a property of the thing praised that is possessed independently of valuation. Praise is not the sort of thing that could properly be applied to everything without becoming empty, as Leibniz says.

Second, Leibniz argues that God's valuing would be arbitrary if it made things good, since God would have no good reason for valuing some things rather than others. There would be nothing to prevent God from valuing snails more than human beings, for instance, or grains of sand more than snails. So God's decision about what kind of world to create could not be informed by facts about the goodness of various possible worlds until God had made the logically prior decision about what kinds of things to value and to what degree. In

---

21 Or perhaps they should be understood as endorsing the Possibility of Complete Intrinsic Value Neutrality described in Chapter 2, Section 2, and positing instead a different kind of value entirely.
22 See Leibniz 1991, *Discourse on Metaphysics*, section 2. Leibniz actually offers a third argument, based upon the book of Genesis, in which God is described as discovering (not deciding) that creation is good, but I shall pass over that one.

short, if there were no measure of goodness independent of God's valuing activity, then there would be no way for God to get things right or wrong, and this seems mistaken. These arguments from Leibniz provide theists with two more good reasons to reject DSIV, reasons that strike me as collectively quite compelling.[23]

2. What Kind of World is This?

Nicholas Everitt develops a novel argument against the existence of God based on the scale of the universe. It is interesting to consider whether the Main Conclusion defended earlier in this book has any bearing on Everitt's argument.

Everitt argues that if God created the world with human beings in mind, then they should have appeared relatively early in history and the universe should be human-scaled in size, roughly as it is depicted in the account of creation in *Genesis*. Of course, the universe is not like this at all. Human beings appeared only recently, and the universe is truly vast and quite hostile to human life in most places. For example, more than 99.999% of the time, there have been no human beings, and most life forms are microscopic; the most distant star is about 20×10^{16} times as far away from us as the sun is, and there are roughly 10^{22} stars in the universe.[24] Everitt wonders why "the universe as it is revealed to us by modern science is *hugely* unlike the sort of universe which the traditional theist would lead us to expect," and argues that in the end, the scale of the universe makes theism improbable.[25]

In response to some possible objections, Everitt points out that although his argument depends on certain assumptions about value, they are assumptions that traditional theists can be expected to share. For instance, traditional theists should admit that all other things being equal, species which are capable of possessing knowledge are better than those that are not capable of this.[26] Given this kind of value judgment, Everitt wonders what purpose God

---

23 As Mark Murphy has pointed out to me in correspondence, though, Leibniz's arguments here do not count against a Platonic account of goodness in terms of participation.
24 See Everitt 2004, Chapter 11, especially pp. 216–17.
25 Everitt 2004, p. 216; see also p. 217ff.
26 Everitt 2004, p. 221.

might have for creating a universe lacking such species nearly everywhere and for such a long time.

Given the Main Conclusion, though, God has a reason to value for its own sake every concrete particular thing that exists. In fact, even if human beings had never existed in the universe, the world would still be a place of immense intrinsic value. So Everitt's argument is significantly weakened, if not completely neutralized, by the intrinsic value of everything.

Of course, his argument gains an air of plausibility from the fact that historically, many traditional theists have been rather anthropocentric about their place in the universe.[27] But surely it is a mistake, from the point of view of traditional theism, to think that the entire material creation revolves around human beings. As St. Augustine says,

> When you observe the differences among material objects and see that some are brighter than others, it would be wrong to want to get rid of the darker ones, or to make them just like the brighter ones. Instead, if you refer them all to the perfection of the whole, you will see that these differences in brightness contribute to the more perfect being of the universe.[28]

Embracing the Main Conclusion would certainly help anthropocentric theists to regain a proper sense of place in the world, theologically speaking, and to help to motivate a concern for the natural environment for its own sake. As Wendell Berry says,

> We have lived by the assumption that what was good for us would be good for the world. We have been wrong. We must change our lives, so that it will be possible to live by the contrary assumption that what is good for the world will be

---

[27] Not always, of course; one thinks of the example of St. Francis of Assisi, for instance. See White 1967 for more on this, along with the suggestion that St. Francis be considered the patron saint of the environment.

[28] St. Augustine 1993, p. 88. The idea that the perfection of the whole universe might be God's focus in creation was developed first by the ancient Stoics (see Jordan, p. 205). The book of Job makes this point forcefully, especially without the extra passage added on to the end of the book.

good for us. We must recover the sense of the majesty of the creation and the ability to be worshipful in its presence. For it is only on the condition of humility and reverence before the world that our species will be able to remain in it.[29]

By way of summary, then, although the existence of God does not suggest that we ought to change the fundamental ontology of intrinsic value, it does make an important difference in terms of explaining the origins of the actual distribution of intrinsic value in the world. In addition, the existence of God makes a difference to the way in which we answer the Distribution Question discussed in Chapter 2 (namely, how much of the world, if any, is intrinsically valuable). In Chapter 4 (Section 5), I argued that the following picture of the distribution of intrinsic value was the most plausible one:

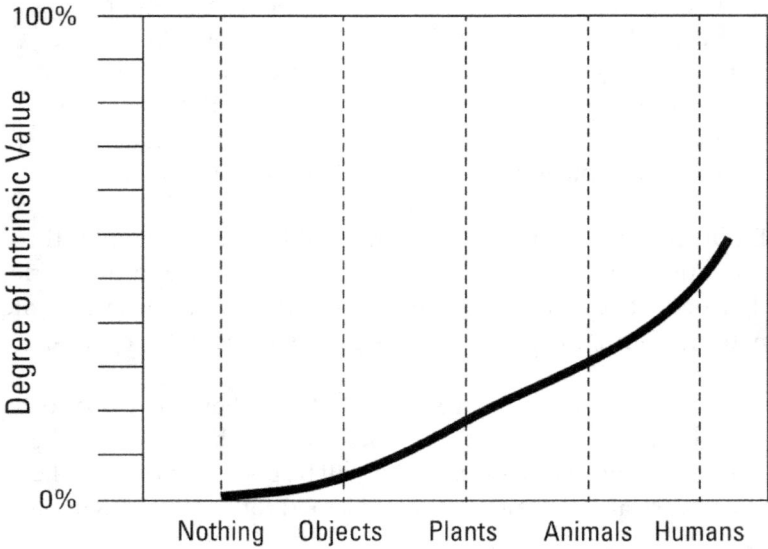

Figure 3 The Possibility of Ubiquitous Intrinsic Value Varying by Degrees

One of my arguments for this conclusion involved comparing it to the next most plausible alternative, namely, Figure 5:

---

29 Berry 2003, p. 196.

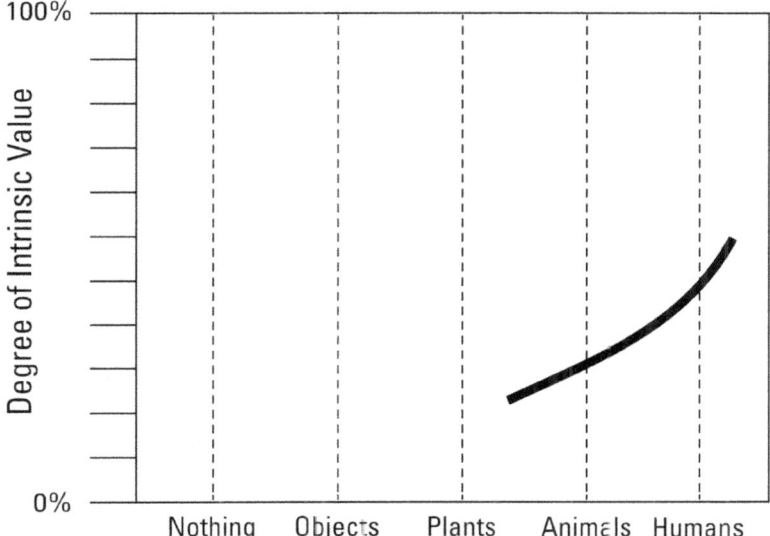

Figure 5 The Possibility of Restricted Intrinsic Value Varying by Degrees

I argued earlier that the view pictured in Figure 3 was simpler than the one pictured in Figure 5, since it did not require a non-arbitrary answer to the Cutoff Question in order to explain why the black line ends abruptly exactly where it does.

According to theists, though, even Figure 3 is inadequate as it stands, since God possesses intrinsically all kinds of properties that make God intrinsically valuable. In fact, traditional theists would insist that not only is God the ideal valuer, as noted above, but also God is that than which none more intrinsically valuable could be conceived, since God alone possesses (essentially and intrinsically) the best possible intrinsic structure.[30] Together with the traditional theistic idea that there are nonhuman creatures "in between" human beings and God, which help to constitute a

---

[30] For more on this idea, which is rooted in St. Anselm's claim that God is "that than which none greater can be conceived," see the essays in Morris 1989 and Nagasawa's argument for the conclusion that Anselmian theism does not commit one to the claim that God is omnipotent, omniscient, and omnibenevolent (Nagasawa 2008) This fact may give non-theists a reason to hope that God exists, since it would be good if something of the highest degree of intrinsic value existed.

Great Chain of Being stretching from nothingness to perfection,[31] we arrive at the following picture (see Figure 6):

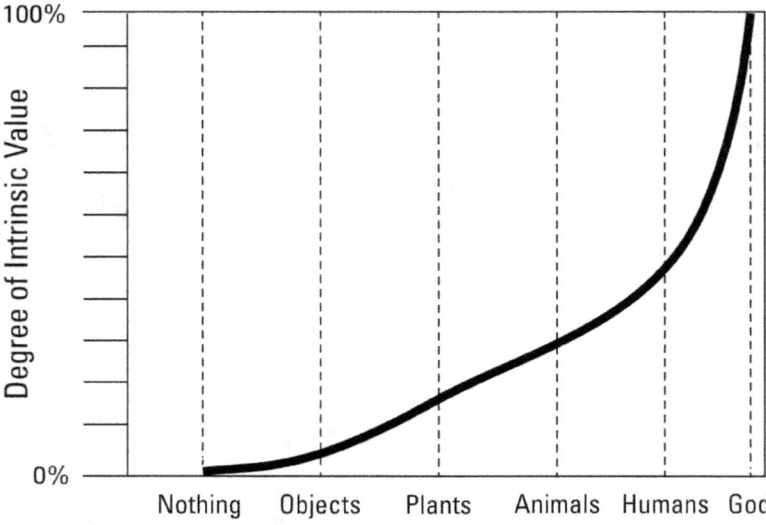

Figure 6 Degrees of Intrinsic Value

This picture has the added advantage, when compared to Figure 3, of answering what might be called the Upward Cutoff Question, namely, "Why does the actual degree of intrinsic value go only so high, and no higher?"[32] In addition, consider those theists who agree that human beings, God, and anything "in between" are intrinsically valuable, but who are uncertain about the Main Conclusion. The symmetry and elegance of Figure 6 is quite striking when compared to the alternative, as depicted in Figure 7:

---

31 One version of this idea can be found in the pagan philosopher Plotinus (see Plotinus 1964), whose Neo-Platonism heavily influenced the medieval theists of all three traditions; for a helpful discussion, see Lovejoy 1976.

32 St. Thomas Aquinas's fourth of his famous five ways of proving the existence of God is based on the intelligibility of this question: see *Summa Theologiae*, Part I, question II, article 3.

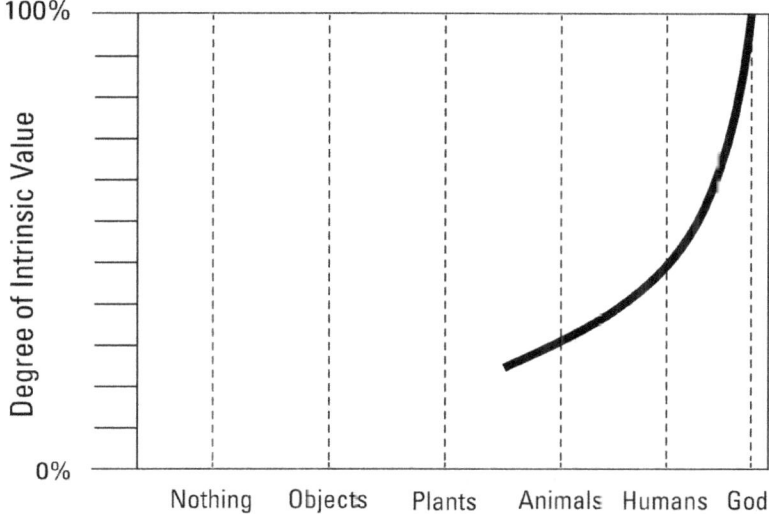

Figure 7 Degrees of Intrinsic Value With a Cutoff Point

For such theists, then, the relative simplicity of Figure 6 over Figure 7 provides an additional reason to embrace the Main Conclusion of this book.

This completes my brief exploration of the ontological relevance of theism to the Main Conclusion of this book. In the remaining section, I shall discuss the relevance of theism to the ethical conclusions developed in Chapter 6.

3. Theism, Ethics, and Intrinsic Value

Some traditional theists have thought that God's existence makes an important difference (sometimes all the difference) to ethics. Many discussions of this topic revolve around the so-called Divine Command Theory, according to which all human ethical obligations are determined by God's commands. Since this is well-worn territory, I shall not discuss it here. Instead, I shall explore the difference that God's existence makes in terms of the activities of gratitude and worship.

In an early draft of Thomas Merton's highly influential autobiography, there appears an interesting passage that never made it into the final manuscript. Contrasting the self-centered love *affectio commodi* with the disinterested love *affectio justitiae* distinguished by John Duns Scotus, Merton says the following:

> Happiness consists only in the freedom of disinterested love – the ability to get away from ourselves, and our own limited sphere of interests and appetites and needs, and rejoice in the good that is in others, not because it is also ours, but formally in so far as it is theirs![33]

I have doubts about Merton's claim that happiness consists *only* in the freedom of disinterested love. His defense of it seems fallacious:

> Is it not obvious that when we have this freedom, happiness will not only follow as a matter of course: joy would pursue us everywhere and we could not get away from it.[34]

The problem here is that just because the freedom of disinterested love is sufficient for happiness, it does not follow that such freedom is also necessary.

However, Merton's explanation of the idea that happiness would follow immediately from disinterested love is very interesting:

> Since everything that is, is good, and since the world is full of things that are good in themselves and which all proclaim the infinite goodness and power of God: if we rejoiced in the good that is possessed by others, formally as possessed by them, we would not be able to look at a flower or a blade of grass or an insect or a drop of water or a grain of sand or a leaf, let alone a whole tree, or a bird, or a living animal, or a human being, without exploding with exultation.[35]

---

33 Merton 1989, p. 316.
34 Merton 1989, p. 316.
35 Merton 1989, p. 316.

As I argued in Chapter 6, part of being an ethically good person is that one be symbolically for the good. And according to the Main Conclusion, with which Merton seems to agree, we are literally surrounded by intrinsic goodness. There is a clear sense in which it would be appropriate, on occasion, to be so sensitive as to lose oneself momentarily in this ubiquitous goodness, and if one is a theist, to be grateful to God for it.

When is gratitude appropriate, in general terms? It seems that it is appropriate for person A to be grateful to person B just in case A believes that B has brought about some good that benefits A and B was not obliged to do this. According to the conjunction of traditional theism and my Main Conclusion, God has freely created a world full of intrinsically valuable things, including you and me, without any obligation to do so.[36] It seems perfectly appropriate to be grateful for the existence of such things, and also for our experiences of them, which are often intrinsically valuable themselves.

By contrast, Everitt argues that the idea of viewing one's life as a gift from God is incoherent. This is because of the fact that "If A is to make a gift to B, then A and B must both already exist." So if we have a duty of gratitude to God, it must be based on "some supposed benefit which God has rendered us after we were already in existence."[37]

Everitt's premise here certainly holds true in the typical case of gift giving, since it is impossible to give a gift to a non-existent person. Of course, God's creation would not be a typical case of gift giving. Imagine that by means of some interesting mechanism, persons were capable of surviving periods of nonexistence followed by the resumption of normal life, and that such interludes of nothingness were routinely accepted as commonplace and not

---

36 Free creation is one earmarks of the traditional theist's account of the relationship between God and the created world; in the early medieval period, it served to distinguish traditional theists from Neo-Platonists, Aristotelians, and others who viewed the world as necessary in itself or as a necessary emanation from the One.
37 Everitt 2004, p. 130.

at all frightful.³⁸ Suppose that you were to enter a period of non-existence, believing that you would reappear at some point in the not-so-distant future, but then you awoke to find that you had not existed for a considerably longer period of time. Imagine finally that you discovered that someone had tried to prevent you from coming back into existence (hence the delay), but someone else succeeded in bringing you back into existence anyway, although later than planned. Would it make sense to be grateful to the person who brought you back into existence, without whose efforts you would have never existed again? I think so.

Some readers will no doubt object to this thought experiment because they do not believe that human life can be interrupted in this way. Such readers should imagine then that the person in the thought experiment comes to agree with their views concerning personal identity and interruption, and so comes to regard his or her apparent memories of the past as false impressions that would be appropriate only for some other person's life. Still, wouldn't it be appropriate for this (new) person to be grateful to the person who brought him or her into existence just recently, without whose efforts he or she would have never existed at all? Again, I think so. Hence it is not incoherent to be grateful for being brought into existence, contrary to Everitt.

Even if this line of response to Everitt is not convincing, the theist could concede his point about the gift of existence and appeal to the fact that according to traditional theism, God sustains everything in being from moment to moment. Wouldn't it make sense to be grateful to God for this? Everitt thinks not:

> So many lives contain so much pain and suffering – negative features which on the face of it God could have prevented. In such a circumstance, it might well seem that resentment is the more appropriate emotion. Even if God has given something

---

38 Nagel appeals to this possibility to argue that non-existence alone is not what makes death bad, although his example involving people who are frozen seems insufficient to me to count as a case of non-existence; see Nagel 1979 and the discussion of harm in Feinberg 1984.

> valuable, if he could so easily have given something so very much more valuable, it is less clear that gratitude is the right emotion. The appropriateness of gratitude is a function not just of the benefit that accrues to the beneficiary, but also of the degree of sacrifice which is made by the benefactor. It is far from clear how much gratitude we owe to someone who has brought us a benefit at no cost to himself, and who could, also with no cost to himself, have brought us a very much greater benefit.[39]

Everitt makes a good point here about sacrifice. We do believe that gratitude is more appropriate, all other things being equal, if the benefactor sacrifices in order to confer the benefit. If someone donates a kidney to a stranger, for instance, we would find ingratitude in the recipient much more outrageous than if a dollar had been donated instead. But is Everitt right to say that it is far from clear how much gratitude we owe to a person who confers a benefit upon us at no cost, and could have conferred a much greater one instead? Is he right to suggest that resentment might be a reasonable emotion in such circumstances?

I don't think so. To return to the human sphere again, if a group of very, very wealthy people were to create a fellowship program for scholars that awarded me a summer grant of ten percent of my annual salary to work on a philosophy book, then I would be very grateful to them for this even if in the end, they ended up coming out even financially because of some tax loophole. I would be more grateful, of course, to a moderately well-off benefactor who sacrificed to fund my research, but that is beside the point: I would still be grateful, and appropriately so, for the benefit conferred by the program created by the very, very wealthy people. It would be beside the point to note that they could have given me much more money instead.

So I conclude that Everitt is wrong to suggest that there is something inappropriate about traditional theists expressing gratitude

---

39 Everitt 2004, p. 130.

toward God for both existence and continued life, given what they believe about God's relationship to creation.[40]

In addition, some of the prominent practices of traditional theists take on a new significance when viewed in light of the Main Conclusion and the ethical position defended in Chapter 6. Offering prayers of thankfulness and engaging in rituals of worship, for instance, can be ways of being symbolically for the good, especially when one is helpless to make direct causal contributions to it in the world (see Chapter 6).[41] Even if the worship of God makes no measurable difference in terms of producing good consequences, it is an important part of being an ethically good person for theists, since it is based upon and expresses the recognition of God's supreme intrinsic value.[42] This concludes my investigation of the relevance of theism to the ethical conclusions defended in Chapter 6.

By way of conclusion, then, although there are good reasons to deny that God is responsible for the intrinsic value in the sense of creating it simply by valuing things for their own sake, traditional theists have every reason to thank God for creating a world containing so many things of intrinsic value. As illustrated by the new diagrams introduced earlier in this chapter, there is a good fit between the Main Conclusion of this book, the ethical position developed in Chapter 6, and traditional theism.

---

[40] See also the discussion of the intrinsic badness of pain and the argument for the conclusion that no concrete particular thing is intrinsically bad, in Chapter 5.

[41] Offering prayers of petition can have the same effect, even if one does not believe that they will be efficacious in the sense of moving God to act: for a discussion of this, see Davison 2009.

[42] See Adams 1999, p. 14.

Bibliography

Adams, Robert M. *Finite and Infinite Goods* (Oxford: Oxford University Press, 1999).
Agar, Nicholas. *Life's Intrinsic Value: Science, Ethics, and Nature* (New York: Columbia University Press, 2001).
Alston, William P. "Religious Experience and Religious Belief," *Nous* 16 (1982), pp. 3–12.
— "Perceiving God," *Journal of Philosophy* 83 (November 1986), pp. 655–65.
— "Epistemic Circularity," *Philosophy and Phenomenological Research* 47 (1986), pp. 1–30; reprinted in *Epistemic Justification: Essays in the Theory of Knowledge* (Ithaca: Cornell University Press, 1989), pp. 319–49.
— *Perceiving God* (Ithaca: Cornell University Press, 1991).
Anderson, Elizabeth. *Value in Ethics and Economics* (Cambridge, MA: Harvard University Press, 1993).
— "Practical Reason and Incommensurable Goods," in Chang, Ruth (ed.), *Incommensurability, Incomparability, and Practical Reason* (Cambridge, MA: Harvard University Press, 1997), pp. 90–109.
St. Anselm. *Proslogion*, translated by S. N. Deane (La Salle, Illinois: Open Court Publishing Company, 1962).
Aquinas, St. Thomas. On Evil, translated by Richard Regan, edited with an introduction by Brian Davies (Oxford University Press, 2003).
Aristotle. *Nicomachean Ethics*, translated by Terence Irwin (Indianapolis, IN: Hackett Publishing Company, 1985).
Artsen, Jan A. "Good as Transcendental and the Transcendence of the Good," in MacDonald, Scott (ed.), *Being and Goodness* (Ithaca, NY: Cornell University Press, 1991), pp. 56–73.
Audi, Robert. "Intrinsic Value and Moral Obligation," *Southern Journal of Philosophy* 35 (1997), pp. 135–54.
— *The Good in the Right: a Theory of Intuition and Intrinsic Value* (Princeton, NJ: Princeton University Press, 2004).
Augustine, St. *On the Free Choice of the Will*, translated by Thomas Williams (Indianapolis, IN: Hackett Publishing Company, 1993).
Aydede Murat (ed.), *Pain: New Essays on Its Nature and the Methodology of Its Study* (Cambridge, MA: MIT Press, 2006).
— "Pain," in Edward N. Zalta (ed.), *The Stanford Encyclopedia of Philosophy*, (Spring 2010 edition). Available online at: <http://plato.stanford.edu/archives/spr2010/entries/pain/>.

Brentlinger, John. "The Nature of Love," in John Brentlinger (ed.), *The Symposium of Plato*, translated by Suzy Q. Gooden (Amherst, MA: University of Massachusetts Press, 1970), pp. 113–29; reprinted in Alan Soble (ed.), *Eros, Agape, and Philia* (St. Paul, MN: Paragon House, 1989), pp. 136–48.

Barnes, Jonathan. "Medicine, Experience and Logic," in Jonathan Barnes, J. Brunschwig, M. F. Burnyeat, and M. Schofield (eds), *Science and Speculation* (Cambridge: Cambridge University Press, 1982).

Baron, Marcia W. "Kantian Ethics," in *Three Methods of Ethics* by Marcia W. Baron, Philip Pettit, and Michael Slote (Oxford: Blackwell Publishers, 1997).

Benatar, David. *Better Never To Have Been: The Harm of Coming Into Existence* (Oxford: Oxford University Press, 2008).

Bergmann, Michael. "Epistemic Circularity: Malignant and Benign," *Philosophy and Phenomenological Research* LXIX(3) (November 2004), pp. 709–27.

— "Epistemic Circularity and Common Sense: A Reply to Reed," *Philosophy and Phenomenological Research* LXXIII(1) (2006), pp. 198–207.

— *Justification Without Awareness: A Defense of Epistemic Externalism* (Oxford: Oxford University Press, 2009).

Bernstein, Mark. "Intrinsic Value," *Philosophical Studies* 102 (2001), pp. 329–43.

— "Marginal Cases and Moral Relevance," *Journal of Social Philosophy* 33(4) (2002), pp. 523–39.

Berry, Wendell. "A Native Hill," *The Long-Legged House* (Shoemaker & Hoard, 2003).

— *Life is a Miracle* (Berkeley: Counterpoint Press, 2001).

Black, Tim. "Contextualism in Epistemology," *Internet Encyclopedia of Philosophy* (July 15, 2006). Available online at: <http://www.iep.utm.edu/contextu/>.

Blackburn, Simon. "Errors and the Phenomenology of Value," in Ted Honderich (ed.), *Morality and Objectivity* (London: Routledge, 1985a).

— "Supervenience Revisited," in Ian Hacking (ed.), *Exercises in Analysis: Essays by Students of Casimir Lewy* (Cambridge: Cambridge University Press, 1985b); reprinted in Sayre-McCord 1988b, pp. 59–75.

Bradley, Ben. "Is Intrinsic Value Conditional?," *Philosophical Studies* 107 (2002), pp. 23–44.

— "Two Concepts of Intrinsic Value," *Ethical Theory and Moral Practice* 9(2) (April 2006), pp. 111–30.

— "Benatar and the Logic of Betterness," *Journal of Ethics & Social Philosophy* (discussion note, March 2010).

Brennan, Andrew. "The Moral Standing of Natural Objects," *Environmental Ethics* 6 (Spring 1984), pp. 5–56.

Brentlinger, John, "The Nature of Love," in Alan Soble (ed.), *Eros, Agape, and Philia: Readings in the Philosophy of Love* (New York: Paragon House, 1989), pp. 136–48.

Brink, David O. "Moral Realism and the Sceptical Arguments," *Australasian Journal of Philosophy* 62(2) (June 1984), pp. 11–25.

Boethius, *De Hebdomadibus* in Arthur Hyman and James Walsh (eds), *Readings in Medieval Philosophy* (Indianapolis: Hackett Publishing, 1983), pp. 114–17.

Boyd, Richard. "How to be a Moral Realist," in Geoffrey Sayre-McCord (ed.), *Essays on Moral Realism* (Ithaca: Cornell University Press, 1988), pp. 187–228.

Broad, C. D. *Five Types of Ethical Theory* (New York: Harcourt Brace, 1930).

Burge, Tyler. "Individualism and the Mental," *Midwest Studies in Philosophy*, 4, Studies in Epistemology (Minneapolis: University of Minnesota Press, 1979), edited by P. French, T. Uehling, and H. Wettstein, pp. 73–121.

Butler, Joseph. *Fifteen Sermons Preached at the Rolls Chapel* (Charlottesville, Virginia: Ibis Publishing, 1987).

Butchvarov, Panayot. *Skepticism in Ethics* (Indianapolis: Indiana University Press, 1989).

Card, Robert F. "Consequentialist Teleology and the Valuation of States of Affairs," *Ethical Theory and Moral Practice* 7(3) (2004), pp. 253–65.

Carter, Robert Edgar. "Comparative Value Theory," *Journal of Value Inquiry* 13 (Spring 1979), pp. 33–56.

Chisholm, Roderick. *Brentano and Intrinsic Value* (New York: Cambridge University Press, 1986).

Clark, Stephen R. L. *The Moral Status of Animals* (Oxford Clarendon Press, 1977).

Clements, Colleen D. "Stasis: The Unnatural Value," *Ethics* 86 (January 1976), pp. 136–43; reprinted in Robert Elliot (ed.), *Environmental Ethics* (Oxford: Oxford University Press, 1995), pp. 215–25.

Conee, Earl. "Instrumental Value Without Intrinsic Value?," in *Philosophia* 11 (July 1982), pp. 345–59.

Chardin, Pierre Teilhard de. *Hymn of the Universe*, translated by Simon Bartholomew (New York: Harper & Row, 1965).

D'Arms, Justin, and Daniel Jacobson. "Sentiment and Value," *Ethics* 110 (2000) pp. 722–48.

Dancy, Jonathan. "The Particularist's Progress," in Brad Hooker and Margaret Little (eds), *Moral Particularism* (Oxford: Clarendon Press, 2000), pp. 130–56.

— "Should We Pass the Buck?," in Anthony O'Hear (ed.), *Philosophy, the Good, the True and the Beautiful* (Cambridge: Cambridge University Press, 2000), pp. 159–73; reprinted in Toni Rønnow-Rasmussen and Michael J. Zimmerman (eds), *Recent Work on Intrinsic Value* (Dordrecht: Springer, 2005), pp. 33–44.

Davidson, Donald. "Knowing One's Own Mind," *Proceedings and Addresses of the American Philosophical Association* 61 (1987), pp. 41–58.

Davison, Scott A. "Could Abstract Objects Depend Upon God?," in *Religious Studies* 27 (December 1991), pp. 485–97.

— (1999a), "Moral Luck and the Flicker of Freedom," *American Philosophical Quarterly* 36(3) (July 1999), pp. 241–51.

— (1999b), "Salvific Luck," *International Journal for Philosophy of Religion* 45(2) (April 1999), pp. 129–37.

— "Petitionary Prayer," in Thomas, P. Flint and Michael Rea (eds), *The Oxford Handbook of Philosophical Theology* (Oxford: Oxford University Press, 2009).

— "A Natural-Law Based Environmental Ethic" *Ethics and the Environment* 14(1) (Spring 2009), pp. 1–13.

DeGrazia, David. *Taking Animals Seriously: Mental Life and Moral Status* (Cambridge: Cambridge University Press, 1996).

Dennett, Daniel. "Why You Can't Make a Computer That Feels Pain," *Synthese* 38(3) ("Automaton-Theoretical Foundations of Psychology and Biology, Part I," July 1978), pp. 415–56.

— *Darwin's Dangerous Idea: Evolution and the Meaning of Life* (New York: Simon & Schuster, 1996).

DeRose, Keith. *The Case for Contextualism: Knowledge, Skepticism, and Context*, Vol. 1 (Oxford: Oxford University Press, 2009).

Draper, Paul. "God and Perceptual Evidence," *International Journal for Philosophy of Religion* 32(3), (December 1992), pp. 149–65.

Elliot, Robert. "Intrinsic Value, Environmental Obligation, and Naturalness," *The Monist* 75(2) (April 1992), pp. 138–60.

Everitt, Nicholas. *The Non-Existence of God* (London: Routledge, 2004).

Ewing, A. C. *The Definition of Good* (London: MacMillan, 1947).

Fara, Michael. "Dispositions," in Edward N. Zalta (ed.), *The Stanford Encyclopedia of Philosophy* (Summer 2009 edition). Available online at: <http://plato.stanford.edu/archives/sum2009/entries/dispositions/>.

Feinberg, Joel. "Problematic Responsibility in Law and Morals," *The Philosophical Review* 71 (1962), pp. 340–51; reprinted in *Doing and Deserving* (Princeton: Princeton University Press, 1970), pp. 25–37.

— *Harm to Others* (Oxford: Oxford University Press, 1984); selections reprinted as "Death and Posthumous Harms" reprinted in John Martin Fischer (ed.), *The Metaphysics of Death* (Stanford, CA: Stanford University Press, 1993), pp. 171–90.

Feldman, Fred. "Hyperventilating about Intrinsic Value," *The Journal of Ethics* 2 (1998), 339–54.
— "Basic Intrinsic Value," *Philosophical Studies* 99 (2000), pp. 319–46.
Finnis, John. *Natural Law and Natural Rights* (Oxford: Oxford University Press, 1980).
Flanagan, Owen. *Varieties of Moral Personality: Ethics and Psychological Realism* (Cambridge: Harvard University Press, 1991).
Flowers, Betty S. "Death, the Bald Scenario," in Robert C. Solomon and Jeff Malpas (eds), *Death and Philosophy* (New York, NY: Routledge, 1998), pp. 50–6.
Forrest, Peter. "Supervenience: The Grand-Property Hypothesis," *Australasian Journal of Philosophy* 66 (March 1988), pp. 1–12.
Frankena, William. *Ethics*, 2nd edn, (Englewood Cliffs, NJ: Prentice-Hall, 1973).
Goodpaster, Kenneth. "On Being Morally Considerable," *The Journal of Philosophy* LXXV(6) (June 1978), pp. 308–25.
Gracia, Jorge. "Evil and the Transcendentality of Goodness," in Scott MacDonald (ed.), *Being and Goodness* (Ithaca: Cornell University Press, 1991).
Gutting, Gary. *What Philosophers Know: Case Studies in Recent Analytic Philosophy* (Cambridge: Cambridge University Press, 2009).
Hare, John E. *The Moral Gap* (Oxford: Oxford University Press, 1996).
Harman, Elizabeth. "Critical Study of *Better Never To Have Been: The Harm of Coming Into Existence*," *Noûs* 43(4) (2009), pp. 776–85.
Hartman, Robert S. *The Structure of Value* (Southern Illinois University Press, 1967).
Heraclitus, *The Cosmic Fragments*, translated by G. S. Kirk (Cambridge: Cambridge University Press, 1954).
Hoffman, Joshua, and Gary S. Rosenkrantz. *Substance among other Categories* (Cambridge: Cambridge University Press, 1994).
Humberstone, L. "Intrinsic/Extrinsic," *Synthese* 108 (1996), pp. 205–67.
Hume, David. *A Treatise of Human Nature*, L. A. Selby-Bigge (ed.) (2nd edn), revised by P. H. Nidditch (Oxford: Oxford University Press, 1987).
Hurka, Thomas. "Two Kinds of Organic Unity," *Journal of Ethics* 2(4) (1998), pp. 299–320.
— "Moore's Moral Philosophy," in Edward N. Zalta (ed.), *The Stanford Encyclopedia of Philosophy* (Spring 2005 edition). Available online at: <http://plato.stanford.edu/archives/spr2005/entries/moore-moral/>.
Hyde, Dominic. "Sorites Paradox," in Edward N. Zalta (ed.), *The Stanford Encyclopedia of Philosophy* (Fall 2008 edition). Available online at: <http://plato.stanford.edu/archives/fall2008/entries/sorites-paradox/>.

Jordan, James N. *Western Philosophy from Antiquity to the Middle Ages* (New York: Macmillan Publishing Company, 1987).
Kagan, Shelly. "Rethinking Intrinsic Value," *Journal of Ethics* 2(4) (1998), pp. 277–97.
Kant, Immanuel. *Critique of Pure Reason* (1787, 2nd edn), translated by Norman Kemp-Smith (London: Macmillan Publishing Company, 1933).
— *Fundamental Principles of the Metaphysics of Morals*, translated by T. K. Abbott (Englewood Cliffs, NJ: Prentice Hall, 1949).
King, Peter. "The Problem of Individuation in the Middle Ages," *Theoria* 66 (2000), pp. 159–84.
Gracia, Jorge L. (ed.), *Individuation in Scholasticism: The Later Middle Ages and the Counter-Reformation 1150–1650* (Albany, NY: State University of New York Press, 1994).
Knapp, Christopher. "Equality and Proportionality," *Canadian Journal of Philosophy* 37(2) (2007), pp. 179–201.
Kohák, Erazim. *The Embers and the Stars* (Chicago: University of Chicago Press, 1984).
Korsgaard, Christine M. "Two Distinctions in Goodness," *The Philosophical Review* XCII(2) (April 1983), pp. 169–95.
Kraut, Robert. "Love De Re," *Midwest Studies in Philosophy* X (1986) pp. 419–30.
Kretzmann, Norman. (1991A), "A General Problem of Creation," in MacDonald 1991A, pp. 208–28.
— (199B), "A Particular Problem of Creation," in MacDonald 1991A, pp. 229–49.
Kripke, Saul. "Identity and Necessity," in Milton Munitz (ed.), *Identity and Individuation* (New York: New York University Press, 1971).
Laird, John. *The Idea of Value* (Cambridge: Cambridge University Press, 1929).
Lammenranta, Markus. "Epistemic Circularity," *Internet Encyclopedia of Philosophy* (May 26, 2011) ISSN 2161-0002. Available online at: <http://www.iep.utm.edu/ep-circ/>.
Langton, Rae, and David Lewis. "Defining 'Intrinsic," *Philosophy and Phenomenological Research* 58(2) (1998), pp. 333–45.
Lee, Stan (writer) and Jack Kirby (illustrator), *The Fantastic Four*, 48, March 1966 (New York, NY: Marvel Comics).
Leibniz, Gottfried Wilhelm. *Discourse on Method and Other Essays*, translated by Daniel Garber and Roger Arew (Indianapolis: Hackett Publishing Company, 1991).
Lemos, Noah. *Intrinsic Value* (Cambridge: Cambridge University Press, 1994).
Lewis, David. *Counterfactuals* (Oxford: Wiley-Blackwell, 1973).

— "Extrinsic Properties," *Philosophical Studies* 44 (1983), pp. 197–200.
— *On the Plurality of Worlds* (Oxford: Basil Blackwell, 1986).
— "Elusive Knowledge," *Australasian Journal of Philosophy* 74(4) (December 1996), pp. 549–67.
Linzey, Andrew. *Animal Theology* (University of Illinois Press, 1995).
Loptson, Peter. "The Antinomy of Death," in Robert, C. Solomon and Jeff Malpas (eds), *Death and Philosophy* (New York, NY: Routledge, 1998), pp. 135–51.
Lovejoy, Arthur. *The Great Chain of Being* (Cambridge, MA: Harvard University Press, 1976).
Lowe, E. J. *The Four-Category Ontology: A Metaphysical Foundation for Natural Science* (Oxford: Clarendon Press, 2006).
— *A Survey of Metaphysics* (Oxford: Oxford University Press, 2002).
MacDonald, Scott. (1991A) (ed.), *Being and Goodness* (Ithaca, NY: Cornell University Press, 1991).
— (1991B), "The Relation Between Being and Goodness," in MacDonald 1991A, pp. 1–28.
— (1991C), "The Metaphysics of Goodness and the Doctrine of the Transcendentals," in MacDonald 1991A, pp. 31–55.
MacIntyre, Alasdair. *Dependent Rational Animals: Why Human Beings Need the Virtues* (London: Duckworth, 1999).
Mackie, J. L. *Ethics: Inventing Right and Wrong* (New York: Penguin Books, 1986).
Merricks, Trenton. *Objects and Persons* (Oxford: Oxford University Press, 2001).
Merton, Thomas. *A Thomas Merton Reader*, Thomas, P. McDonnell (ed.) (New York: Image Books, 1989).
Mill, John Stuart. *Utilitarianism* in James, M. Smith and Ernest Sosa (eds), *Mill's Utilitarianism: Text and Criticism* (Belmont, CA: Wadsworth, 1969).
Moore, G. E. *Principia Ethica* (Cambridge: Cambridge University Press, 1903).
— *Ethics* (New York: Henry Holt and Company, 1912).
— "The Concept of Intrinsic Value," in *Philosophical Studies* (London: Routledge and Kegan Paul Ltd., 1960).
Morris, Thomas V. *The Logic of God Incarnate* (Ithaca: Cornell University Press, 1986).
— (ed.), *The Metaphysics of Theism* (Ithaca: Cornell University Press, 1988).
— *Anselmian Explorations* (Notre Dame, IN: University of Notre Dame Press, 1989).
Motokawa, Tatsuo. "Sushi Science and Hamburger Science," *Perspectives in Biology and Medicine* 32 (1989), pp. 489–504.

Murphy, Mark. *Natural Law and Practical Rationality* (Cambridge: Cambridge University Press, 2001).

Nagasawa, Yujin. "A New Defence of Anselmian Theism," *The Philosophical Quarterly* 58(233) (October 2008), pp. 577–96.

Nagel, Thomas. (1976), "Moral Luck," *Proceedings of the Aristotelian Society* 50(Supplementary Volume, 1976), pp. 137–51; reprinted in *Mortal Questions* (Cambridge: Cambridge University Press, 1979), pp. 24–38.

— "Death," in *Mortal Questions* (Cambridge: Cambridge University Press, 1979); reprinted in John Martin Fischer (ed.), *The Metaphysics of Death* (Stanford, CA: Stanford University Press, 1993), pp. 61–9.

— *The View from Nowhere* (Oxford: Oxford University Press, 1986).

Nash, Roderick Frazier. *The Rights of Nature: A History of Environmental Ethics* (Madison, Wisconsin: University of Wisconsin Press, 1989).

Norton, Bryan. "Epistemology and Environmental Values," *The Monist* 75(2) (April 1992), pp. 208–26.

Nozick, Robert. *Philosophical Explanations* (Cambridge: Harvard University Press, 1981).

Okakura, Kazuko. *The Book of Tea* (Tokyo: Kenkyusha, 1962).

Olson, Jonas. "Revisiting the Tropic of Value: Reply to Rabinowicz and Rønnow-Rasmussen," *Philosophy and Phenomenological Research* 67(2) (Summer 2003), pp. 412–22.

O'Neill, John. "The Varieties of Intrinsic Value," *The Monist* 75(2) (April 1992), pp. 119–137; reprinted in Heimir Geirsson and Michael Losonsky (eds), *Beginning Metaphysics* (Hoboken: Blackwell Publishers, 1998), pp. 105–22.

Passmore, John. "Attitudes To Nature," in R. S. Peters (ed.), *Nature and Conduct* (New York: St. Martin's Press, 1975), pp. 251–64; reprinted in Robert Elliot (ed.), *Environmental Ethics* (Oxford: Oxford University Press, 1995), pp. 129–41.

Pini, Giorgio. "The Individuation of Angels from Bonaventure to Duns Scotus," in *A Companion to Angels in the Middle Ages*, Tobias Hoffmann (ed.) (Leiden and Boston: Brill publishing company, 2012).

Plantinga, Alvin. *The Nature of Necessity* (Oxford: Oxford University Press, 1974).

Plato. *Apology* in *Five Dialogues*, trans G. M. A. Grube (Indianapolis, IN: Hackett Publishing Company, 1981).

Plotinus. *The Essential Plotinus*, translated by Elmer O'Brien (Indianapolis, IN: Hackett Publishing Company, 1964).

Putnam, Hilary. "The Meaning of 'Meaning'," in K. Gunderson (ed.), *Language, Mind and Knowledge, Minnesota Studies in the Philosophy of Science* 7 (Minneapolis, MN: University of Minnesota Press, 1975).

Quine, W. V. O. "On What There Is," in *From a Logical Point of View* (Cambridge, MA: Harvard University Press, 1953), pp. 1–19.
Rabinowicz, W. and Rønnow-Rasmussen, T. "A Distinction in Value: Intrinsic and For Its Own Sake," *Proceedings of the Aristotelian Society* 100 (1999), pp. 33–51.
— "The Strike of the Demon: On Fitting Pro-Attitudes and Value," *Ethics* 114 (2004), 391–423.
Rachels, James. *Created from Animals: The Moral Implications of Darwinism* (Oxford: Oxford University Press, 1990).
Regan, Tom. "The Case for Animal Rights," in Peter Singer (ed.), *In Defense of Animals* (Oxford: Basil Blackwell, Inc., 1985), pp. 13–26.
— "Does Environmental Ethics Rest on a Mistake?," *The Monist* 75(2) (April 1992), pp. 161–82.
Rescher, Nicholas. *Introduction to Value Theory* (Washington, DC: University Press of America, 1982).
Rolston III, Holmes. *Environmental Ethics: Duties To and Values In the Natural World* (Philadelphia: Temple University Press, 1988).
— *Conserving Natural Value* (New York: Columbia University Press, 1994).
Ross, W. D. *The Right and the Good* (Oxford: Oxford University Press, 1930).
Routley, Richard and Val Routley. "Against the Inevitability of Human Chavinism," in Kenneth Goodpaster and Kenneth Sayre (eds), *Ethics and the Problems of the 21st Century* (Notre Dame: University of Notre Dame Press, 1979), pp. 36–59; reprinted in Robert Elliot (ed.), *Environmental Ethics* (Oxford: Oxford University Press, 1995), pp. 104–28.
Russell, Bertrand. "On Denoting," *Mind* (new series), 14 (1905), pp. 479–93.
— *A History of Western Philosophy* (London: George Allen & Unwin Ltd., 1946).
Rysiew, Patrick. "Epistemic Contextualism," in Edward N. Zalta (ed.), *Stanford Encyclopedia of Philosophy* (September 7, 2007). Available online at: <http://plato.stanford.edu/entries/contextualism-epistemology/>.
Sacks, Oliver. *The Man Who Mistook His Wife for a Hat and Other Clinical Tales* (New York: Simon & Schuster, 1985).
Sandbach, F. H. *The Stoics* (London: Chatto & Windus, 1975).
Sayre-McCord, Geoffrey. "Moral Theory and Explanatory Impotence," *Midwest Studies in Philosophy* (University of Minnesota Press, 1988a), 12, pp. 433–57; reprinted in Sayre-McCord 1988b, pp. 256–81.
— *Essays on Moral Realism* (Ithaca: Cornell University Press, 1988b).

— "The Many Moral Realisms," in Geoffrey Sayre-McCord (ed.), *Essays on Moral Realism* (Ithaca: Cornell University Press, 1988c).
Scanlon, Thomas. *What We Owe to Each Other* (Cambridge, MA: Harvard University Press, 1998).
Schroeder, Mark. "Value Theory," in Edward N. Zalta (ed.), *The Stanford Encyclopedia of Philosophy* (Fall 2008 edition). Available online at: <http://plato.stanford.edu/archives/fall2008/entries/value-theory/>.
Seuss, Dr. *Horton Hears a Who!* (New York: Random House, 1954).
Sider, Theodore. "Intrinsic Properties," *Philosophical Studies* 83 (1996), pp. 1–27.
— "Maximality and Microphysical Supervenience," *Philosophy and Phenomenological Research* 66 (2003), pp. 139–49.
Singer, Peter. *Animal Liberation* (New York: Avon Books, 1977); reprinted in John Arthur (ed.), *Morality and Moral Controversies* (Englewood Cliffs, NJ: Prentice-Hall, 1981).
Sober, Elliott. "Putting the Function back into Functionalism," in William Lycan (ed.), *Mind and Cognition: A Reader* (Oxford: Basil Blackwell, 1990), pp. 63–70.
— "Philosophical Problems for Environmentalism," in B. Norton (ed.), *The Preservation of Species* (Princeton: Princeton University Press, 1986), pp. 173–95; reprinted in Robert Elliot (ed.), *Environmental Ethics* (Oxford: Oxford University Press, 1995), pp. 226–47.
Spiegel, James. *Hypocrisy: Moral Fraud and Other Vices* (Grand Rapids, Michigan: Baker Books, 1999).
Stalnaker, Robert. "A Theory of Conditionals," *Studies in Logical Theory, American Philosophical Quarterly Monograph* 2 (1968), pp. 98–112.
Stump, Eleonore and Norman Kretzmann. "Being and Goodness," in MacDonald 1991A, pp. 98–128.
Sturgeon, Nicholas L. "Anderson on Reason and Value," *Ethics* 106(3) (1996), pp. 509–24.
Swinburne, Richard. *Providence and the Problem of Evil* (New York: Oxford University Press, 1998).
Thomasson, Amie. "Categories," in Edward N. Zalta (ed.), *The Stanford Encyclopedia of Philosophy* (Fall 2010 edition). Available online at: <http://plato.stanford.edu/archives/fall2010/entries/categories/>.
Topmiller, Robert J. "Most Venerable Thich Quang Duc" (August 1999). Available online at: <http://www.quangduc.com/English/vnbuddhism/013quangduc.html>.
Tolhurst, William. "On the Nature of Intrinsic Value," *Philosophical Studies* 43 (May 1983), pp. 383–96.
Tännsjö, Törbjorn. "A Concrete View of Intrinsic Value," *Journal of Value Inquiry* 33(4) (December 1999), pp. 531–36.

Taylor, Paul W. "The Ethics of Respect for Nature," *Environmental Ethics* 3 (Fall 1981), pp. 197–218.

Thompson, Janna. "A Refutation of Environmental Ethics," *Environmental Ethics* 12(2) (Summer 1990), pp. 147–60.

Vallentyne, Peter. "Intrinsic Properties Defined," *Philosophical Studies* 88 (1997), pp. 209–19.

Van Inwagen, Peter. *Material Beings* (Ithaca, NY: Cornell University Press, 1990).

Vander, David Laan. "Counterpossibles and Similarity," in Frank Jackson (ed.), *Lewisian Themes: The Philosophy of David K. Lewis* (Oxford: Clarendon Press, 2004), pp. 258–75.

Varner, Gary E. *In Nature's Interests?: Interests, Animal Rights, and Environmental Ethics* (New York: Oxford University Press, 1998).

Vlastos, Gregory. "The Individual as an Object of Love in Plato," in Gregory Vlastos, *Platonic Studies* (Princeton: Princeton University Press, 1973), reprinted in Alan Soble (ed.), *Eros, Agape, and Philia* (St. Paul, MN: Paragon House, 1989), pp. 96–135.

von Wright, G. H. *The Varieties of Goodness* (London: Routledge and Kegan Paul, 1963).

Walhout, Donald. *The Good and the Realm of Values* (Notre Dame: University of Notre Dame Press, 1978).

Wasserman, Ryan. "Material Constitution," in Edward N. Zalta (ed.), *The Stanford Encyclopedia of Philosophy* (Spring 2009 edition). Available online at: <http://plato.stanford.edu/archives/spr2009/entries/material-constitution/>.

Watkins, Michael. *Rediscovering Colors*, Philosophical Studies series Vol. 88 (Norwell, MA: Kluwer Academic Publishers, 2002).

Watson, Gary. "Free Agency," *Journal of Philosophy* lxxii(8) (April 1975), pp. 205–20; reprinted in Gary Watson (ed.), *Free Will* (Oxford: Oxford University Press, 1982), pp. 96–110.

Weatherson, Brian. "Intrinsic vs. Extrinsic Properties," in Edward N. Zalta (ed.), *The Stanford Encyclopedia of Philosophy* (Spring 2007 edition). Available online at: <http://plato.stanford.edu/archives/spr2007/entries/intrinsic-extrinsic/>.

— "The Asymmetric Magnets Problem," *Philosophical Perspectives* 20 (2006), pp. 479–92.

Westacott, Emrys. "Some Objections to an Objectivist Conception of Intrinsic Value," *Southwest Philosophy Review* 10(1) (January 1994), pp. 177–86.

White Jr., Lynn. "The Historical Roots of Our Ecological Crisis," *Science* 3767 (March 1967), pp. 1203–7; reprinted in Donald VanDeVeer and Christine Pierce (eds), *The Environmental Ethics & Policy Book*, 2nd edn, (Wadsworth Publishing Company, 1998), pp. 48–54.

Wolter, Allan B. "John Duns Scotus," *The Encyclopedia of Philosophy*, Vol. 1 (New York: MacMillan Publishing Co., Inc. and The Free Press, 1967).

Wolterstorff, Nicholas. "The World Ready-Made," in Terence Cuneo (ed.) *Practices of Belief: Selected Essays*, Vol. 2 (Cambridge: Cambridge University Press, 2010), pp. 12–40.

— "Does the Role of Concepts Make Experiential Access to Ready-Made Reality Impossible?," in Terence Cuneo (ed.), *Practices of Belief: Selected Essays*, Vol. 2 (Cambridge: Cambridge University Press, 2010), pp. 41–61.

Wright, Crispin. "On the coherence of vague predicates," *Synthese* 30(3–4) (1975), pp. 325–65.

Zagzebski, Linda. "What If the Impossible Had Been Actual?," in Michael, D. Beaty (ed.), *Christian Theism and the Problems of Philosophy* (Notre Dame, IN: University of Notre Dame Press, 1990).

Zimmerman Michael J. *The Nature of Intrinsic Value* (Lanham, Maryland: Rowman and Littlefield Publishers, 2001).

— "Intrinsic vs. Extrinsic Value," in Edward N. Zalta (ed.), *The Stanford Encyclopedia of Philosophy* (Winter 2010 edition). Available online at: <http://plato.stanford.edu/archives/win2010/entries/value-intrinsic-extrinsic/>.

Index

Adams, Robert M. 12n. 8, 12n. 9, 21n. 45, 24n. 56, 29n. 4, 37n. 20, 43n. 29, 45n. 1, 50n. 14, 51n. 16, 66–8, 74, 82, 89, 92n. 35, 105n. 25, 105n. 27, 108, 109n. 38, 110n. 41, 111n. 44, 118–20, 132n. 42
Agar, Nicholas 66n. 11, 70–1, 73, 84–5, 87n. 25, 100–1, 106–8
agent-neutral 94
agent-relative 94, 95
Alston, William 22–4
ambitious speculative conclusion 19, 45–59, 79, 88–97
Anaximander 79–81
Anaximenes 79
Anderson, Elizabeth 12n. 10, 28n. 1, 45n. 1, 50–3, 56, 89, 90n. 30, 108n. 36
animals 3, 6, 20, 28–30, 50, 61, 65–8, 82, 84–5, 107, 111n. 44, 128
annihilation 24, 35–6, 52, 61, 71–4, 77, 79, 87
Anselm, St. 20n. 42
anthropocentrism 64–6, 104, 112, 123
Anything is Better than Nothing argument 47n. 9, 71–2, 73–4, 87, 91
archaeon 83–4

Aristotle 12n. 7, 51, 64, 80, 83, 94n. 41, 103n. 17, 129n. 36
Artsen, Jan A. 80n. 4
Audi, Robert 105
Augustine, St 5, 7, 80–1, 88, 95, 101, 123
Aydede, Murat 94n. 44

Benjamin Davison vii, 34, 118, 120
Bentham, Jeremy 72, 94n. 41
Bergmann, Michael vii, 22n. 49, 119n. 15
Bernstein, Mark 41n. 22, 66n. 13, 87, 103–4, 105n. 25, 105n. 26
Berry, Wendell 2n. 2, 112n. 47, 123–4
Black, Tim 22n. 49
Blackburn, Simon 15n. 22, 16n. 29
Boethius 117–19
Boyd, Richard 16n. 29
Bradley, Ben vii, 10n. 3, 17n. 32, 28n. 1, 29n. 4, 31n. 8, 36n. 17, 45, 49n. 12, 50n. 15, 64n. 8, 104n. 22
brains 65, 82, 85
Brentano, Franz 103
Brentlinger, John 53, 54n. 27, 116, 117n. 5
Broad, C. D. 14
buck-passing 15–16, 42–3
Buddhism 111
Butchvarov, Panayot 51

Card, Robert 50n. 15, 53n. 24

Index

Carter, Robert E. 10n. 3, 17n. 30, 24–5, 35n. 16, 103n. 19, 112n. 47
challenge argument 75
Chisholm, Roderick 14, 45n. 1, 46, 49n. 11, 85n. 17, 89, 93n. 37, 103
Clark, Stephen 102
colors 9, 16n. 26
complexity 71, 72, 83n. 12
conclusion, ambitious speculative 19, 45–59, 79, 88–97
conclusion, main 1, 2, 3, 5, 7, 10, 19, 20, 25n. 58, 26, 27, 32n. 10, 41, 46, 55, 58, 59, 61, 62, 64, 71, 75–8, 79, 82, 86–9, 97, 99, 102, 113, 115, 122–7, 129, 132
Conee, Earl 103n. 17
corpses 3–4
creation 74–5, 111n. 44, 116, 117, 121, 122, 123, 124, 129, 132
criteria 24, 33–7, 82, 97, 99–103
cutoff question 26, 27, 28, 29n. 4, 30–3, 38, 41, 43, 59, 61–78, 79, 100, 105n. 26, 125, 126

Dancy, Jonathan 15n. 25, 63n. 4, 105n. 27
D'Arms, Justin 13n. 13
Davies, Brian 88n. 26
Davison, Scott A. 81n. 6, 110n. 42, 116n. 4, 132n. 41
DeGrazia, David 66n. 11
degree question 27–32
demarcation problem 100
Dennett, Daniel 94n. 44, 102n. 13
DeRose, Keith 22n. 49
Dewey, John 17n. 30
dignity 65–6
Diotima of Mantinea 51
distribution question 27, 32, 38, 39, 41, 62, 64, 76, 110, 121, 124

Divine Subjectivism about Intrinsic Value (DSIV) 116–22
Draper, Paul 23n. 51
Duc, Thich Quang 110
duplicate 17–18, 35n. 15, 57n. 42, 35, 89n. 29
duty 6n. 8, 12, 14, 74, 75, 105, 108, 110, 129
egalitarianism 29n. 4, 66–7

Elliot, Robert 17n. 30
epistemic circularity 22
epistemological seriousness 21–5
equality 67
essentiality 18
ethical seriousness 9, 10, 26, 99n. 1, 102, 113
Euthyphro 115, 119
Everitt, Nicholas 122–4, 129–32
excellence of persons 67–8, 82n. 10, 118–20
existence 20
explanation question 27, 28, 32, 33, 41–3

Fara, Michael 57n. 41
Feinberg, Joel 110n. 42, 130n. 38
Feldman, Fred 10n. 3, 16n. 29, 18n. 37, 102–3
Flanagan, Owen 12n. 8, 106, 108
Flint, Thomas P. vii
Flowers, Betty S. 37n. 20
Forrest, Peter 16n. 29
Francis, St. 107n. 33, 123n. 27
Frankena, William 11n. 6, 12n. 8

Galactus 87n. 24
Geach, Peter 12n. 8
Genesis 111n. 44, 121n. 22, 122
Gettier, Edmund 2

God 13n. 12, 22, 23, 26, 29n. 6, 67, 76n. 39, 80, 85n. 15, 86n. 20, 115–32
Goggans, Philip vii, 62n. 2
good 1, 4, 6, 7, 10–4, 69–73, 80, 81, 86, 88n. 6, 101, 108, 113, 115, 117–22, 128, 129, 132
Goodpaster, Kenneth 69–72
Grace Davison vii, 34, 84
Gracia, Jorge 81n. 8, 86n. 21
gratitude, 110n. 42, 127–31
Gutting, Gary 2, 13n. 14, 75

Hall, Everett 53–4
Hankinson, Amanda vii
Hartman, Robert 81n. 7, 86
Heraclitus 3
Hoffman, Joshua 89n. 28
human-centered 3, 4, 5, 69
Humberstone, L. 15n. 24
Hume, David 15n. 22
Hurka, Thomas 12n. 8, 17n. 30, 43n. 27
Hyde, Dominic 62, 64n. 5
hypocrisy 7, 112–13

incommensurability 58
incorruptibility 18
inherent value 28, 29, 68
inherent worth 69, 101
intrinsic property 16–18, 55, 83–4
intrinsic structure 18, 20–1, 24, 35, 42, 58, 63, 71, 72n. 30, 74, 77, 82–6
intrinsic value,
 and abstract entities 46–51, 88–94
 bearers of 46–59
 characterized 4, 10–14
 and criteria 24, 33–7, 82, 97, 99–103
 degrees of 19, 28–32, 79–86
 epistemology of 21–5
 and existence 20
 and God 115–32
 ground of 14–18
 and intrinsic properties 16–18
 and intrinsic structure 18, 20–1, 24, 35, 42, 58, 63, 71, 72n. 30, 74, 77, 82–6
 and necessity 18–19
 objectivity of 15–16, 42–3
 possible distribution of 32–41
 and reasons for acting 5–6, 7, 104–14
intrinsically bad 45, 49, 71n. 28, 86–8, 93, 94–6, 104, 132n. 40

Jackson, Frank 57n. 41
Jackson, Michael 4
Jacobson, Daniel 13n. 13
Jesus 116, 117n. 6
Job 123n. 28
Jordan, Mark 79n. 1, 80n. 2, 123n. 28

Kagan, Shelly 10n. 3, 17, 54–5
Kant, Immanuel 6n. 8, 15n. 23, 20n. 42, 55, 64–6
King, Peter 81n. 8
Knapp, Christopher 29n. 4, 64n. 6
Kohák, Erazim 24n. 55
Korsgaard, Christine 10, 11, 17n. 30, 35n. 16, 54
Kraut, Robert 53
Kretzmann, Norman 80n. 4, 81n. 5, 118n. 9
Kripke, Saul 2

Laird, John 103n. 19
Langton, Rae 17n. 33
Leibniz, Gottfried Wilhelm von 121–2
Lemos, Noah 14n. 16, 16n. 29, 18n. 37, 45n. 1, 46–53, 56, 57n. 40, 85n. 17, 89, 93n. 37, 93n. 38

148 Index

Lewis, David 17n. 33, 22n. 49, 32n. 9
Lincoln, Abraham 17, 54
Loptson, Peter 34–5, 61n. 1
Losonsky, Michael vii, 14n. 18
Lovejoy, Arthur 126n. 31
Lowe, E. J. 18n. 35, 89n. 28

MacDonald, Scott 80n. 4, 86n. 21, 115n. 2, 117n. 7
machines 66, 70–2, 104, 106–7
MacIntyre, Alasdair 66n. 11
Mackie, John L. 12n. 8, 15n. 22, 16n. 29
main conclusion 1, 2, 3, 5, 7, 10, 19, 20, 25n. 58, 26, 27, 32n. 10, 41, 46, 55, 58, 59, 61, 62, 64, 71, 75–8, 79, 82, 86–9, 97, 99, 102, 113, 115, 122–7, 129, 132
maximization 74, 108
Mellema, Gregory vii
Merricks, Trenton 20n. 43, 20n. 44
Merton, Thomas 127–9
Mill, John Stuart 23, 94n. 41, 99n. 1
Moore, G. E. 12n. 8, 14, 16, 43, 85n. 17, 87n. 24, 99n. 1, 103
morally defective 7, 112
Murphy, Mark vii, 13n. 14, 43n. 29, 72n. 30, 81n. 6, 105n. 26, 122n. 23

Nagasawa, Yujin vii, 20n. 42, 25n. 58, 62n. 2, 125n. 30
Nagel, Thomas 15n. 22, 15n. 24, 37n. 20, 37n. 21, 43, 94, 96, 102n. 11, 110n. 42, 130n. 38
Nash, Roderick 106
Neo-Platonism 117, 126n. 31, 129n. 36
Norton, Bryan 1n. 1
Nozick, Robert 14n. 18, 23, 42n. 26, 82n. 10, 85n. 17
Nygren, Anders 116, 117n. 6

O'Brien, Wendell vii
Okakura, Kazuko 111
O'Neill, John 12n. 10, 14, 16, 17n. 30, 20n. 43, 86–7, 104
ontological seriousness 9, 10, 16, 78
organic disunity 96
organic unity 42n. 26, 58, 85

pain 51, 69, 72, 88, 94–6, 130, 132n. 40
Pargetter, Robert 57n. 41
Passmore, John 64n. 7
perception 21, 22, 23, 84
persuasive elaboration 2, 25
Pini, Giorgio 81n. 8
Plantinga, Alvin 46n. 5, 47n. 6, 91n. 33, 93n. 38, 118n. 8
plants 3, 6, 21, 61, 66, 82, 85, 100
Plato 12n. 8, 24n. 56, 47, 50, 51, 54, 64, 80, 94n. 41, 108, 109n. 38, 115, 117, 118, 122n. 23, 126n. 31, 129n. 36
pleasure 23, 47, 48, 49, 51, 54–5, 69, 72
Plotinus 126n. 31
Prior, Elizabeth 57n. 41
properly functioning valuer 13, 15, 20, 24, 35, 36, 42, 52, 61, 63, 71, 74, 82, 95, 105, 109, 116, 118
Putnam, Hilary 15n. 23, 119n. 16

Quine, W. V. O. 2, 13n. 14, 91n. 32

rabbit 84
Rabinowicz, Wlodek 12n. 10, 13, 17n. 30, 45n. 2, 54, 56, 82n. 9, 108n. 36
Rachels, James 66n. 11
reasons, conclusive 6, 99
reasons, overridable 6–7, 99, 104, 107, 108
Regan, Tom 28, 30, 68–9, 105

Rescher, Nicholas 81n. 7, 86–7, 103n. 17
resemblance to God 67–8, 82n. 10, 118–20, 118–20
respect 3–7, 50, 64, 99, 103–14
rocks 20, 74, 82, 87, 112
Rolston III, Holmes 17n. 30
Rønnow-Rasmussen, Toni 12n. 10, 13, 17n. 30, 45n. 2, 54, 56, 82n. 9, 108n. 36
Rosenkrantz, Gary S. 89n. 28
Ross, W. D. 15, 46n. 4, 46n. 5, 85n. 17, 103, 105n. 27
Routley, Richard 66n. 12, 75n. 38, 100n. 4, 103n. 17
Routley, Val 66n. 12, 75n. 38, 100n. 4, 103n. 17
Russell, Bertrand 20n. 42
Rysiew, Patrick 22n. 49

Sacks, Oliver 65n. 10, 82n. 11
sand 7, 82, 121, 128
Sayre-McCord, Geoffrey 12n. 8, 15n. 22, 43n. 27
Scanlon, Thomas P. 12n. 8, 15–16, 42, 108–9
Schroeder, Mark 63n. 4
Scotus, John Duns 95n. 47, 128
semantic seriousness 9, 10
sentience 72, 95, 96, 102
Seuss, Dr. 73n. 35
Sider, Theodore, 17n. 33, 18n. 34, 35n. 15
Silver Surfer 87n. 24
simplicity 2, 58, 62, 77, 79, 127
Singer, Peter 72–4
Sober, Elliot 1n. 1, 41n. 22, 70n. 27, 100
Socrates 1
sorites paradox 62–4
speciesism 34, 105
Spiegel, James 113n. 48
Stalnaker, Robert 32n. 9

Stoics 123n. 28
Stump, Eleonore 81n. 5
Sturgeon, Nicholas 50n. 15
Suarez, Francisco 86n. 21
subjectivism about value 14
Swinburne, Richard 85n. 17
symbolic goodness 108–13, 129, 132
Symposium 50, 51n. 16

T4 virus 87n. 25
Täännsjö, Törbjorn 45n. 1, 92
Taylor, Paul W. 69, 70n. 24
Thales 79
Thomas, St. 12n. 7, 80–1, 86n. 21, 88, 126n. 32
Thomasson, Amie 89n. 28
Thompson, Jana 100
Thomson, Judith Jarvis 12n. 8
Tolhurst, William 17n. 30, 35n. 16
Topmiller, Robert J. 110n. 43
Twaddell, Gerald vii

universality 18
universe 1, 82, 84, 86, 122–3

Vallentyne, Peter 17n. 33
value,
   economic 1, 4, 13, 34
   holism 63
   instrumental 4, 10, 11, 13, 17, 29, 70, 71, 87, 104, 107, 111, 112n. 46
   intrinsic *see* intrinsic value
   neutrality 32–7, 38, 77, 121n. 21
   sentimental 1, 4, 13, 17
   Vander Laan, David 32n. 9
Varner, Gary E. 66n. 11
viruses 7, 31, 66, 86–7, 104
von Wright, G. H. 69n. 23

Walhout, Douglas 25n. 57, 81n. 6, 86n. 21, 115n. 3

Wang, Yafeng vii
Wasserman, Ryan 18n. 35
Watkins, Michael 9, 16n. 26
Watson, Gary 11
Weatherson, Brian 15n. 24, 17n. 30, 17n. 33, 20n. 44, 35n. 15
Weir, Jack vii
Westacott, Emrys 33–7, 99n. 2
White, Lynn Jr. 64n. 7, 107n. 33, 123n. 27
Wolter, Allan B. 95n. 47
Wolterstorff, Nicholas 15n. 23
Wright, Crispin 62n. 3, 69n. 23

Wu, Mowen vii

Xu, Yingjin vii, 71n. 29

Yan, Mengyao vii
Yang, Xi vii

Zagzebski, Linda 32n. 9
Zimmerman, Michael J. vii, 10n. 4, 11n. 6, 12n. 8, 12n. 10, 14, 16n. 29, 17n. 32, 18n. 37, 45n. 1, 45n. 2, 46n. 4, 46n. 5, 49n. 11, 51, 53n. 25, 54–8, 64n. 8, 85n. 17, 89, 94n. 41

www.ingramcontent.com/pod-product-compliance
Lightning Source LLC
Chambersburg PA
CBHW061841300426
44115CB00013B/2472